Weightwatchers

Quick, easy and tasty recipes

Rice & Noodles

First published in Great Britain by Simon & Schuster UK Ltd, 2012
A CBS Company

Copyright © 2012, Weight Watchers International, Inc.
Simon & Schuster Illustrated Books, Simon & Schuster UK Ltd,
First Floor, 222 Gray's Inn Road, London WC1X 8HB

www.simonandschuster.co.uk

Simon & Schuster Australia, Sydney
Simon & Schuster India, New Delhi

Weight Watchers, **ProPoints** and the **ProPoints** icon are the registered trademarks
of Weight Watchers International Inc and are used under licence by Weight Watchers
(UK) Ltd.

Weight Watchers Publications: Cheryl Jackson, Jane Griffiths,
Selena Makepeace, Nina McKerlie and Imogen Prescott.

Recipes written by: Sue Ashworth, Sue Beveridge, Tamsin Burnett-Hall,
Cas Clarke, Siân Davies, Roz Denny, Nicola Graimes, Becky Johnson, Kim Morphew,
Joy Skipper, Penny Stephens and Wendy Veale as well as Weight Watchers Leaders
and Members.

Photography by: Iain Bagwell, Steve Baxter, Steve Lee, Juliet Piddington and
William Shaw.
Project editor: Nicki Lampon.
Design and typesetting: Geoff Fennell.

Colour reproduction by Dot Gradations Ltd, UK
Printed and bound in China.

A CIP catalogue for this book is available from the British Library

ISBN 978-0-85720-931-3

1 2 3 4 5 6 7 8 9 10

Pictured on the title page: Chicken laksa p16
Pictured on the Introduction: Egg fried rice p168, Chinese chillied monkfish p170,
Chicken tikka masala p114.

WeightWatchers®

Quick, easy and tasty recipes

Rice & Noodles

SIMON &
SCHUSTER
ILLUSTRATED

London · New York · Sydney · Toronto · New Delhi

A CBS COMPANY

Weight Watchers **ProPoints** Weight Loss System is a simple way to lose weight. As part of the Weight Watchers **ProPoints** plan you'll enjoy eating delicious, healthy, filling foods that help to keep you feeling satisfied for longer and in control of your portions.

Ⓥ This symbol denotes a vegetarian recipe and assumes that, where relevant, free range eggs, vegetarian cheese, vegetarian virtually fat free fromage frais, vegetarian low fat crème fraîche and vegetarian low fat yogurts are used. Virtually fat free fromage frais, low fat crème fraîche and low fat yogurts may contain traces of gelatine so they are not always vegetarian. Please check the labels.

❄ This symbol denotes a dish that can be frozen. Unless otherwise stated, you can freeze the finished dish for up to 3 months. Defrost thoroughly and reheat until the dish is piping hot throughout.

Recipe notes

Egg size: Medium sized, unless otherwise stated.

Raw eggs: Only the freshest eggs should be used. Pregnant women, the elderly and children should avoid recipes with eggs that are not fully cooked or raw.

All fruits and vegetables: Medium sized, unless otherwise stated.

Stock: Stock cubes are used in recipes, unless otherwise stated. These should be prepared according to packet instructions.

Recipe timings: These are approximate and meant to be guidelines. Please note that the preparation time includes all the steps up to and following the main cooking time(s).

Microwaves: Timings and temperatures are for a standard 800 W microwave. If necessary, adjust your own microwave.

Low fat spread: Where a recipe states to use a low fat spread, a light spread with a fat content of no less than 38% should be used.

Low fat soft cheese: Where low fat soft cheese is specified in a recipe, this refers to soft cheese with a fat content of less than 5%.

Contents

Introduction

Rice & Noodles – staple foods that are in almost everyone's kitchen cupboard but often get overlooked. With the help of recipes from the best of Weight Watchers cookbooks, discover the many fantastic ways of using these two core ingredients.

From soups and salads to family favourites and dishes that are perfect for a special meal, rice and noodles are perfect for any occasion. Try beautiful and unusual risottos such as Salmon Risotto Cakes, or pick a fresh fast stir fry like Sizzling Beef Noodles or Vegetable Chow Mein. For a special meal, why not impress your guests with Tuna and Wild Rice Bake or Stuffed Acorn Squash.

Whatever you choose, all the recipes are easy to prepare, and with the help of Weight Watchers you'll find yourself cooking perfect *Rice & Noodles* every time.

About Weight Watchers

For more than 40 years Weight Watchers has been helping people around the world to lose weight using a long term sustainable approach. Weight Watchers successful weight loss system is based on four tried and trusted principles:

- Eating healthily
- Being more active
- Adjusting behaviour to help weight loss
- Getting support in weekly meetings

Our unique ***ProPoints*** system empowers you to manage your food plan and make wise recipe choices for a healthier, happier you. To find out more about Weight Watchers and the ***ProPoints*** values for these recipes contact Customer Services on 0845 345 1500.

Cooking hints and tips

To cook perfect rice, put the rice in a lidded saucepan, add roughly twice the amount of water and bring to the boil. Reduce the heat, cover and simmer until the rice is cooked. The time this takes will depend on the type of rice you are using, but the water should be all or mostly absorbed, holes should have formed on the surface of the rice and the rice should be tender. Turn off the heat, drain if necessary, replace the lid and leave to stand for a couple of minutes to steam dry. Brown rice takes a little longer to cook than white rice, as does wild rice.

For a perfect risotto, always use risotto rice. The recipes in this book use Arborio rice, but if you cannot find it, use Carnaroli or Vialone Nano rice. All of these are grown specifically for making risottos and will give you the creamy texture that makes a risotto special. To cook risotto rice, add to any ingredients already in the pan and stir fry until translucent, without letting it brown. Now add the stock or liquid as specified in the recipe, adding a ladleful

at a time and stirring until each ladleful is absorbed. Keep adding the liquid, a little at a time, until the rice is cooked. Although you can add all the liquid at once and it will still taste OK, it is this gradual absorption that makes a true risotto.

Noodles are super fast to cook and can even be bought ready cooked in straight to wok packets or found fresh in the chilled vegetable section of large supermarkets. Follow the instructions on the packet as each type has a slightly different cooking time. Ready cooked or fresh noodles will just need heating through.

Shopping hints and tips

White and brown, easy cook or long grain, basmati and risotto – there are so many different types of rice it can be confusing. Here are some guidelines:

- Longer grains tend to remain separate on cooking and so are better for serving as a side dish or in a salad, biryani or pilaff for example
- Shorter grains, such as risotto rice (or pudding rice) tend to stick together more on cooking
- Easy cook rice has already been parboiled, making it harder to over cook it
- White rice is just brown rice that has had the brown skin (husk) removed in the milling process
- Basmati rice is a long grain with a subtle aromatic flavour that goes perfectly with Indian dishes
- Jasmine rice cooks to a slightly sticky texture that is delicately flavoured and ideal with Far Eastern dishes

Many of the noodle recipes in this book use egg noodles, made with wheat flour. These come in various thicknesses, from fine to thick, and can be bought dried, ready prepared or fresh. Other types of noodles include udon noodles, which are thick Japanese wheat noodles, and rice noodles, made from rice. These can be thick and flat or very fine (vermicelli noodles). All are available as dried or ready prepared in most major supermarkets.

We've added a checklist here for common store cupboard ingredients. Just add fresh ingredients and you'll be ready to cook the delicious recipes in *Rice & Noodles*.

Store cupboard checklist

- [ ] artichokes, canned in water
- [ ] artificial sweetener
- [ ] bay leaves
- [ ] black eyed beans, canned
- [ ] cardamom pods
- [ ] chick peas, canned
- [ ] chilli (powder and flakes)
- [ ] chilli sauce
- [ ] Chinese five spice
- [ ] cinnamon sticks
- [ ] coconut essence
- [ ] coconut milk, reduced fat
- [ ] coconut, dessicated
- [ ] cooking spray, calorie controlled
- [ ] coriander (ground and seeds)
- [ ] cornflour
- [ ] crabmeat, canned
- [ ] creamed coconut
- [ ] cumin (ground and seeds)
- [ ] curry leaves, dried
- [ ] curry paste
- [ ] curry powder
- [ ] fennel seeds
- [ ] fish sauce
- [ ] garam masala
- [ ] garlic purée
- [ ] ginger
- [ ] herbs, dried
- [ ] hoisin sauce
- [ ] honey, runny
- [ ] kaffir lime leaves
- [ ] kidney beans, canned
- [ ] lentils, dried
- [ ] mushroom soup, condensed
- [ ] mushrooms, dried porcini
- [ ] noodles (dried or straight to wok)
- [ ] oil (vegetable or olive)
- [ ] olives, in brine
- [ ] oyster sauce
- [ ] paprika
- [ ] peppercorns
- [ ] peppers, piquante
- [ ] raisins
- [ ] rice wine
- [ ] rice, dried
- [ ] saffron
- [ ] salmon, canned red
- [ ] salt
- [ ] seaweed sheets
- [ ] sesame seeds
- [ ] sherry, dry
- [ ] soy sauce
- [ ] stock cubes
- [ ] sugar, caster
- [ ] sultanas
- [ ] sunflower seeds
- [ ] sweetcorn, canned
- [ ] Tabasco sauce
- [ ] tandoori spice mix
- [ ] teriyaki sauce
- [ ] tomato ketchup
- [ ] tomato purée
- [ ] tomatoes, canned
- [ ] tuna, canned in brine
- [ ] turmeric
- [ ] vinegar (white wine and rice)
- [ ] wasabi paste
- [ ] water chestnuts, canned
- [ ] Worcestershire sauce

Soups and salads

Spicy beef noodle soup

Serves 4

377 calories per serving

Takes 10 minutes to prepare +
30 minutes marinating,
35 minutes to cook

225 g (8 oz) lean beef steak, sliced thinly

250 g (9 oz) dried fine egg noodles

200 g (7 oz) sugar snap peas, mange tout or green beans, sliced lengthways

a small bunch of fresh coriander, chopped, to garnish (optional)

For the marinade

1 tablespoon soy sauce

1 garlic clove, crushed

1 cm (½ inch) fresh root ginger, grated

1 tablespoon honey

1 small red chilli, de-seeded and chopped finely

For the soup

2 litres (3½ pints) chicken stock

1 garlic clove

1 lemongrass stem, chopped roughly, or 1 tablespoon dried lemongrass, chopped

1 small red chilli

1 star anise

1 cm (½ inch) fresh root ginger, crushed

This recipe is inspired by the clear, fragrant noodle soups found all over South East Asia, and it makes a very filling lunch.

1 Mix all the marinade ingredients together in a shallow bowl and add the beef strips, stirring to coat thoroughly. Leave to marinate for 30 minutes.

2 Meanwhile, place all the soup ingredients in a large saucepan, bring to the boil and simmer for 30 minutes.

3 Bring a saucepan of water to the boil, add the noodles and cook according to the packet instructions. Drain and place in the bottom of four serving bowls.

4 Heat a non stick frying pan until very hot and brown the marinated beef on all sides. Remove from the pan and set aside.

5 Strain the soup into a clean pan and bring back to a simmer. Add the sugar snap peas, mange tout or green beans and simmer for 2 minutes.

6 Pile the beef on top of the noodles in the bowls, pour the soup over and serve sprinkled with the coriander, if using.

Variation... See page 21 for a fantastic seafood version of this spicy soup.

Chicken laksa

Serves 4
289 calories per serving
Takes 30 minutes

calorie controlled cooking
  spray
2 garlic cloves, crushed
2 teaspoons Thai red or green
  curry paste
400 g (14 oz) skinless boneless
  chicken breasts, cut into
  small pieces
3 tablespoons soy sauce
300 ml (10 fl oz) chicken stock
100 g (3½ oz) dried fine egg or
  rice noodles, broken up
1 teaspoon caster sugar
1 lemongrass stem, chopped
  into 4 pieces and crushed
  slightly
5 kaffir lime leaves, rolled up
  and sliced finely crossways
2 tablespoons low fat coconut
  milk

To garnish
20 g (¾ oz) roasted peanuts,
  chopped
a small bunch of fresh
  coriander, chopped

*A laksa is a Malaysian soupy noodle curry made with a
dizzying array of ingredients.*

1 Heat a wok or large non stick frying pan, spray with the
cooking spray and fry the garlic until golden brown, adding a
splash of water if it starts to stick. Add the curry paste and
stir fry for 30 seconds.

2 Add the chicken pieces and stir briefly until thoroughly
coated with the paste. Add the soy sauce, stock, noodles
and sugar and cook for a further 2 minutes.

3 Add the lemongrass and lime leaves. Lower the heat and
simmer for 10 minutes.

4 Remove the lemongrass pieces and stir in the coconut
milk. Spoon into dishes to serve, garnished with the peanuts
and coriander.

Tip... Thai curry paste is hot and spicy, so adjust the amount
to your liking.

Chinese noodle soup

Serves 2

277 calories per serving

Takes 10 minutes to prepare,
  10 minutes to cook

calorie controlled cooking
  spray

a bunch of spring onions or
  1 small onion, chopped finely

1 garlic clove, sliced finely

2.5 cm (1 inch) fresh root
  ginger, chopped finely

1 small green cabbage
  (e.g. Chinese leaf or Savoy),
  shredded finely

1 carrot, peeled and sliced
  finely

a handful of bean sprouts or
  spinach, chopped

100 g (3½ oz) dried egg or rice
  noodles

600 ml (20 fl oz) vegetable
  stock

a pinch of Chinese five spice

1 tablespoon soy sauce

a pinch of dried chilli flakes
  (optional)

A soothing flavoursome soup that just hits the spot.

1 Spray a large, lidded, non stick saucepan with the cooking spray and gently fry the onions, garlic and ginger for 1 minute. Add a splash of water if they start to stick.

2 Add the vegetables, noodles, stock, Chinese five spice, soy sauce and chilli flakes, if using, cover and bring to the boil.

3 Turn down the heat, simmer for 5 minutes and then serve.

Variation... For a meatier soup, add 4 rashers of lean back bacon, sliced into strips, and stir fry together with the onion, garlic and ginger.

Chicken noodle soup

Serves 2 (as a main meal soup)
297 calories per serving
Takes 25 minutes

1.2 litres (2 pints) hot chicken
   stock
1 garlic clove, chopped, or
   1 teaspoon garlic purée
1 lemongrass stem, sliced
   paper thin
½ level teaspoon ground ginger
300 g (10½ oz) skinless
   boneless chicken breasts,
   cut into strips
1 red chilli, de-seeded and
   chopped
75 g (2¾ oz) shiitake or button
   mushrooms, sliced
4 spring onions, halved
   lengthways and cut into
   5 cm (2 inch) strips
50 g (1¾ oz) dried medium egg
   noodles
1 tablespoon fish sauce
4 tablespoons chopped fresh
   coriander

For those of us who enjoy a taste of the exotic, help is at hand since so many ingredients are now widely available.

1 Pour the hot stock into a large lidded saucepan. Add the garlic, lemongrass and ginger. Cover and simmer.

2 Meanwhile, dry fry the chicken in a non stick pan for 5 minutes. Add the chilli, mushrooms and spring onions and stir fry for a further 5 minutes.

3 Drop the noodles into the simmering stock and cook for 3–4 minutes. Add the chicken mixture and fish sauce. Heat through to allow the flavours to mingle. Stir in the coriander and serve.

Variation... See page 22 for a tasty pork version of this noodle soup.

Spicy prawn noodle soup

Serves 4

361 calories per serving

Takes 10 minutes to prepare
 + 30 minutes marinating,
 35 minutes to cook

225 g (8 oz) raw peeled king or tiger prawns, defrosted if frozen

250 g (9 oz) dried fine egg noodles

200 g (7 oz) sugar snap peas, mange tout or green beans, sliced lengthways

a small bunch of fresh coriander, chopped, to garnish (optional)

For the marinade

1 tablespoon soy sauce

1 garlic clove, crushed

1 cm (½ inch) fresh root ginger, grated

1 tablespoon honey

1 small red chilli, de-seeded and chopped finely

For the soup

2 litres (3½ pints) fish stock

1 garlic clove

1 lemongrass stem, chopped roughly, or 1 tablespoon dried lemongrass, chopped

1 small red chilli

1 star anise

1 cm (½ inch) fresh root ginger, crushed

This is a wonderful seafood version of the recipe on pages 14–15.

1 Mix all the marinade ingredients together in a shallow bowl and add the prawns, stirring to coat thoroughly. Leave to marinate for 30 minutes.

2 Meanwhile, place all the soup ingredients in a large saucepan, bring to the boil and simmer for 30 minutes.

3 Bring a saucepan of water to the boil, add the noodles and cook according to the packet instructions. Drain and place in the bottom of four serving bowls.

4 Heat a non stick frying pan until very hot. Add the prawns and marinade and cook the prawns until they turn pink and are cooked through. Remove from the pan and set aside.

5 Strain the soup into a clean pan and bring back to a simmer. Add the sugar snap peas, mange tout or green beans and simmer for 2 minutes.

6 Divide the prawns equally between the bowls of noodles, pour the soup over and serve sprinkled with the coriander, if using.

Tip... It is well worth taking the time to simmer the stock for this soup, as it brings out all the rich flavours of the herbs and spices.

Pork noodle soup

Serves 2 (as a main meal soup)
391 calories per serving
Takes 25 minutes

1.2 litres (2 pints) hot vegetable stock
1 garlic clove, chopped
1 lemongrass stem, sliced paper thin
½ level teaspoon ground ginger
300 g (10½ oz) lean pork, visible fat removed, cut into strips
1 red chilli, de-seeded and chopped
75 g (2¾ oz) shiitake or button mushrooms, sliced
4 spring onions, halved lengthways and cut into 5 cm (2 inch) strips
50 g (1¾ oz) dried medium egg noodles
1 tablespoon fish sauce
4 tablespoons chopped fresh coriander

This is a wonderful pork version of the Chicken noodle soup on page 19.

1 Pour the hot stock into a large lidded saucepan. Add the garlic, lemongrass and ginger. Cover and simmer.

2 Meanwhile dry fry the pork in a non stick pan for 5 minutes. Add the chilli, mushrooms and spring onions and stir fry for a further 5 minutes.

3 Drop the noodles into the simmering stock and cook for 3–4 minutes. Add the pork mixture and fish sauce. Heat through to allow the flavours to mingle. Stir in the coriander and serve.

Tip... Garlic, chilli, lemongrass and ginger are all available ready prepared in small jars. Once opened, they will keep in the refrigerator for up to 6 weeks.

Fruity rice salad

Serves 4

297 calories per serving

Takes 10 minutes to prepare,
  15 minutes to cook

150 g (5½ oz) dried long grain
  rice

1 teaspoon finely grated lemon
  zest

2 tablespoons lemon juice

1 tablespoon walnut or hazelnut
  oil

1 red apple, cored and chopped

25 g (1 oz) sultanas or raisins

100 g (3½ oz) seedless green
  grapes

100 g (3½ oz) seedless red
  grapes

1 banana, sliced

25 g (1 oz) chopped walnuts

The nut oil adds a lovely flavour.

1 Bring a saucepan of water to the boil, add the rice and cook for about 12 minutes or according to the packet instructions.

2 Meanwhile, mix together the lemon zest, lemon juice and walnut or hazelnut oil in a large serving bowl. Add all the fruit and mix together gently.

3 Drain the rice, rinse with cold water and drain again thoroughly. Add to the fruit and stir to mix. Sprinkle with the walnuts and serve.

Variation... For added crunch, add a couple of sticks of chopped celery.

Turkey and mango noodle salad

Serves 4
416 calories per serving
Takes 25 minutes

125 g (4½ oz) dried vermicelli
noodles
a kettleful of boiling water
calorie controlled cooking
spray
4 garlic cloves, chopped finely
400 g (14 oz) turkey mince
2.5 cm (1 inch) fresh root
ginger, chopped finely
1–2 small red chillies,
de-seeded and chopped finely
a bunch of spring onions,
chopped finely
juice of 2 limes
4 tablespoons soy sauce
100 ml (3½ fl oz) vegetable
stock
2 ripe mangoes, peeled, stoned
and sliced
a small bunch of fresh
coriander, chopped
a few sprigs of fresh mint,
chopped
2 Little Gem lettuces, shredded
4 lime wedges, to serve

*The mango gives this salad a fresh taste and fantastic
colour.*

1 Place the noodles in a boil, cover with boiling water and
leave to soak for 5 minutes or according to the packet
instructions. Drain and chop roughly with scissors.

2 Heat a wok or large non stick frying pan and spray with
the cooking spray. Stir fry the garlic for a few seconds, until
golden, and then fry the turkey for 4 minutes until browned,
breaking it up with a wooden spoon.

3 Add the ginger, chillies, spring onions, noodles, lime juice,
soy sauce and vegetable stock. Stir together and heat through
for 2 minutes.

4 Remove from the heat and stir through the mango, coriander
and mint. Place a pile of lettuce on each serving plate or
bowl and spoon on the noodles. Serve with lime wedges to
squeeze over.

Eastern prawn salad

Serves 4

194 calories per serving

Takes 10 minutes to prepare,
20 minutes to cook

125 g (4½ oz) dried brown
  basmati rice

300 g (10½ oz) cooked peeled
  tiger prawns

100 g (3½ oz) cherry tomatoes,
  halved

220 g can whole water
  chestnuts in water, drained
  and quartered

2 tablespoons chopped fresh
  coriander

grated zest and juice of
  2 limes

2 teaspoons Chinese five spice

a generous pinch of dried chilli
  flakes

100 g (3½ oz) fine green beans,
  trimmed and cut in half

This will last for 2 days in the fridge. Serve with
¼ x 90 g (3¼ oz) bag of prawn crackers per person.

1 Bring a large saucepan of water to the boil, add the
rice and cook for 20 minutes or according to the packet
instructions.

2 Meanwhile, in a large bowl stir together the prawns,
tomatoes, water chestnuts, coriander, lime zest and juice,
Chinese five spice and chilli flakes. Set aside.

3 Add the green beans to the rice and cook for the final
minute. Drain and rinse in cold water. Drain again, ensuring
it is drained thoroughly.

4 Stir the rice and beans into the prawns and serve
immediately.

Chicken with noodles

Serves 4
260 calories per serving
Takes 45 minutes

200 g (7 oz) dried glass noodles
calorie controlled cooking
  spray
2 garlic cloves, sliced thinly
2.5 cm (1 inch) fresh root
  ginger, grated
200 g (7 oz) skinless boneless
  chicken breast, sliced thinly
2 tablespoons light soy sauce
1 tomato, quartered, de-seeded
  and sliced
2 celery sticks, sliced thinly
4 spring onions, sliced thinly
1 green pepper, de-seeded and
  chopped finely
juice of 2 limes
2 small green chillies,
  de-seeded and chopped finely
2 teaspoons caster sugar
a small bunch of fresh
  coriander, chopped
salt and freshly ground black
  pepper

This warm salad is a fantastic variation of the Oriental noodle salad on page 30.

1 Put the noodles into a large bowl, cover with water and leave to soak for 30 minutes or according to the packet instructions. Drain well and snip them with scissors into shorter lengths.

2 Heat a large non stick frying pan and spray with the cooking spray. Stir fry the garlic and ginger for a few seconds. Add the chicken and stir fry for 5 minutes or until the chicken is cooked through and golden.

3 Add the soy sauce, stir fry for a further 30 seconds and then pour everything from the pan over the noodles. Add all the remaining ingredients, toss together, season and then serve.

Tip... Glass noodles are very thin rice noodles that need soaking in cold water for 30 minutes rather than cooking. They can be found in some supermarkets or in Asian food stores.

Wild rice salad

Serves 4

294 calories per serving

Takes 10 minutes to prepare,
30 minutes to cook

**125 g (4½ oz) dried brown
basmati rice**

125 g (4½ oz) dried wild rice

**100 g (3½ oz) mange tout or
sugar snap peas**

1 tablespoon sunflower seeds

1 tablespoon sesame seeds

2 courgettes, grated

**a small bunch of fresh parsley,
chopped**

**a small bunch of fresh
coriander, chopped**

4 spring onions, chopped

**1 red pepper, de-seeded and
chopped finely**

For the dressing

2 tablespoons soy sauce

juice of a lemon

1 teaspoon Tabasco sauce

*This recipe is for four servings, but if you only need one or
two you can keep it in the refrigerator and have it again
the next day. It's also great for a lunchbox.*

1 Bring a large saucepan of water to the boil, add the rice
and cook for 25–30 minutes until the grains are tender, or
according to the packet instructions. Drain and leave to cool.

2 Meanwhile, bring a second saucepan of water to the boil
and blanch the mange tout or sugar snap peas for 30 seconds.
Drain and set aside.

3 Heat a non stick frying pan, add the sunflower and sesame
seeds and toast until golden (be careful not to let them burn).
Add these to all the other salad ingredients, including the
cooked rice, mange tout or sugar snap peas, in a large bowl.

4 Put all the dressing ingredients in an empty jam jar with
a screw top lid, shake well and pour over the salad. Toss
everything together and serve or keep, covered, in the
refrigerator for up to 2 days.

Variation... For a quicker alternative, use white basmati
rice, which cooks in 10 minutes.

Oriental noodle salad

Serves 4
268 calories per serving
Takes 20 minutes

200 g (7 oz) dried vermicelli
   noodles
a kettleful of boiling water
calorie controlled cooking
   spray
2 garlic cloves, sliced thinly
2.5 cm (1 inch) fresh root
   ginger, grated
200 g (7 oz) lean pork
   tenderloin, sliced thinly
2 tablespoons light soy sauce
1 tomato, quartered, de-seeded
   and sliced
2 celery sticks, sliced thinly
4 spring onions, sliced thinly
1 green pepper, de-seeded and
   chopped finely
juice of 2 limes
2 small green chillies,
   de-seeded and chopped finely
2 teaspoons caster sugar
a small bunch of fresh
   coriander, chopped
salt and freshly ground black
   pepper

*This is a very pretty salad that makes a satisfying lunch.
It's also ideal as an accompaniment to an Oriental meal.*

1 Put the noodles into a large bowl, cover with boiling water
and leave to soak for 5 minutes or according to the packet
instructions. Drain well and snip them with scissors into
shorter lengths.

2 Heat a large non stick frying pan and spray with the cooking
spray. Stir fry the garlic and ginger for a few seconds. Add
the pork and stir fry for 5 minutes or until the pork is cooked
through and golden.

3 Add the soy sauce, stir fry for a further 30 seconds and
then pour everything from the pan over the noodles. Add all
the remaining ingredients, toss together, season and then
serve.

Variations... Any kind of noodle could be used for this salad
– just cook according to the packet instructions and then
follow the recipe instructions from step 2.

For a delicious chicken version, see page 28

Tandoori lamb with warm rice salad

Serves 4
513 calories per serving
Takes 20 minutes + marinating

300 g (10½ oz) low fat natural
   yogurt
2 garlic cloves, crushed
2.5 cm (1 inch) fresh root
   ginger, grated finely
2 teaspoons ground turmeric
2 teaspoons garam masala
2 teaspoons ground coriander
400 g (14 oz) lean lamb fillets
200 g (7 oz) dried rice
juice of a lemon
a small bunch of fresh
   coriander, chopped
a small bunch of fresh mint,
   chopped
a bunch of spring onions,
   chopped finely
100 g (3½ oz) mixed salad and
   herb leaves
4 ripe tomatoes, diced
salt and freshly ground black
   pepper

*The lamb in this recipe could be cooked on a barbecue for
that unique smoky flavour.*

1 Mix together the yogurt, garlic, ginger, turmeric, garam
masala and ground coriander, add the lamb and toss to
coat thoroughly. Cover and chill for at least 5 minutes, but
overnight is preferable.

2 Bring a saucepan of water to the boil, add the rice and
cook according to the packet instructions.

3 Preheat the grill to medium-high and line the grill pan
with foil. Grill the lamb for 5–7 minutes on each side until
just cooked through and browned. Remove to a plate, cover
with foil and allow to rest for a few minutes.

4 Meanwhile, drain the rice and mix with the lemon juice,
herbs, spring onions, salad leaves and tomatoes. Season.
Cut the lamb into slices and serve warm with the rice salad.

Wonderful risottos

Pea and herb risotto

Serves 4
332 calories per serving
Takes 40 minutes

850 ml (1½ pints) vegetable
stock

250 g (9 oz) frozen petit pois

4 tablespoons chopped fresh
mint

4 tablespoons chopped fresh
parsley

calorie controlled cooking
spray

1 large onion, chopped finely

1 leek, chopped finely

2 large garlic cloves, chopped
finely

240 g (8½ oz) dried Arborio
risotto rice

150 ml (5 fl oz) dry white wine

salt and freshly ground black
pepper

15 g (½ oz) grated Parmesan
cheese, to serve

This delicious summery dish can also be made with fresh peas when in season.

1 Heat the stock in a saucepan and add half of the petit pois. When cooked, scoop the petit pois out using a slotted spoon and transfer to a food processor, or use a hand held blender, with a small ladleful of stock and the herbs. Whizz until puréed and set aside.

2 Spray a large, lidded, heavy based, non stick saucepan with the cooking spray and fry the onion and leek, half covered, for 9 minutes or until softened – adding a splash of water if they start to stick. Add the garlic and fry for another minute.

3 Add the rice and stir until coated in the onion mixture. Pour in the wine and bring to the boil. Reduce the heat and simmer until the wine is absorbed and the smell of alcohol disappears.

4 Add a ladleful of stock and simmer, stirring, until it is absorbed. Continue to add the stock a ladleful at a time until the liquid is almost fully absorbed and the rice is tender and creamy in texture; this will take 20–25 minutes.

5 Stir in the pea purée and the rest of the peas and heat through. Season and serve sprinkled with the Parmesan.

Chicken and thyme risotto

Serves 4

420 calories per serving

Takes 30 minutes to prepare,
20–25 minutes to cook

❄

1 tablespoon olive oil

1 onion, chopped

1 garlic clove, crushed

125 g (4½ oz) fennel bulb, thinly
shredded

400 g (14 oz) skinless boneless
chicken breasts, diced

275 g (9½ oz) dried Arborio
risotto rice

100 ml (3½ fl oz) dry white wine

850 ml (1½ pints) chicken stock

2 teaspoons fresh thyme

salt and freshly ground black
pepper

To achieve a traditional creamy risotto, serve it straight away; if you leave it sitting around too long the rice becomes a little stodgy.

1 Heat the oil in a large, heavy based, non stick frying pan and add the onion, garlic, fennel and chicken. Stir fry for 5 minutes, until the chicken is sealed on all sides, stir in the rice and cook for 2 minutes.

2 Add the wine and cook until all the liquid has evaporated. Gradually add the stock, a ladleful at a time and cook, stirring, until the rice is tender and the stock has been absorbed. This will take 20–25 minutes.

3 Season to taste and sprinkle in the thyme. Serve immediately.

Tip... Fennel is now widely available in supermarkets – it is a bulb shaped vegetable with a texture similar to celery and it has a subtle aniseed flavour.

Variation... If you find the flavour of fennel too strong, use 4 celery sticks, sliced, instead.

Salmon risotto cakes

Serves 4

232 calories per serving

Takes 40 minutes + cooling

❄

200 g (7 oz) dried Arborio risotto rice

225g (8 oz) mushrooms, chopped finely

1 garlic clove, chopped

3 shallots, chopped finely

700 ml (1¼ pints) vegetable stock

100 g (3½ oz) canned red salmon, drained and flaked

1 tablespoon chopped fresh tarragon

calorie controlled cooking spray

salt and freshly ground black pepper

Using rice rather than the usual mashed potato in these fish cakes adds a unique and tasty twist to a traditional recipe.

1 Place the rice, mushrooms, garlic, shallots and 150 ml (5 fl oz) of the stock in a large saucepan and cook gently, stirring, until the stock has been absorbed. Gradually add the remaining stock, a ladleful at a time, and cook until all the stock has been absorbed and the rice is tender. This will take 20–25 minutes.

2 Allow the rice mixture to cool and then mix in the flaked salmon and tarragon and season. Using wet hands, shape the mixture into eight cakes.

3 Heat a heavy based non stick frying pan and spray with the cooking spray. Cook the risotto cakes for 3–4 minutes on each side until golden. You may need to do this in batches. Serve them warm, allowing two cakes per person.

Variation... Try using the same amount of canned tuna in brine instead of the salmon.

Wild mushroom risotto

Serves 4

415 calories per serving

Takes 30 minutes to prepare,
   30 minutes to cook

**20 g (¾ oz) dried mushrooms
   (e.g. porcini)**

150 ml (5 fl oz) boiling water

**calorie controlled cooking
   spray**

1 onion, chopped finely

2 garlic cloves, crushed

**350 g (12 oz) dried Arborio
   risotto rice**

100 ml (3½ fl oz) white wine

**200 g (7 oz) button mushrooms,
   sliced**

**1.2 litres (2 pints) hot vegetable
   stock**

**a small bunch of fresh parsley,
   chopped**

**salt and freshly ground black
   pepper**

**50 g (1¾ oz) Parmesan cheese,
   grated finely, to serve**

Wild mushrooms give this risotto a rich flavour.

1 Place the dried mushrooms in a measuring jug and add the boiling water. Leave to soak for 25 minutes.

2 Heat a large saucepan, spray with the cooking spray and stir fry the onion and garlic until softened, adding a splash of water if they start to stick.

3 Add the rice, stir to mix well and then add the wine. Drain the reconstituted mushrooms, reserving the soaking liquid, and chop into small pieces. Strain the soaking liquid through a fine mesh sieve or piece of muslin and add to the risotto with the reconstituted and fresh mushrooms.

4 Add the stock in small quantities, cooking and stirring frequently until all of it has been absorbed.

5 Check the seasoning and stir in the parsley. Serve with the Parmesan cheese sprinkled over the top.

Tip... When cooking risotto rice, add the stock a ladleful at a time, making sure each quantity has been absorbed before adding more.

Roasted butternut squash risotto with Gorgonzola and sage

Serves 4
366 calories per serving
Takes 35 minutes

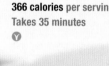

450 g (1 lb) butternut squash, peeled, de-seeded and chopped into even medium size chunks

4 garlic cloves, skins on

calorie controlled cooking spray

10 sage leaves, 8 left whole and 2 chopped finely

300 g (10½ oz) dried Arborio risotto rice

1.2 litres (2 pints) hot vegetable stock

60 g (2 oz) Gorgonzola cheese, crumbled

salt and freshly ground black pepper

Butternut squash is deliciously sweet and goes well with a piquant cheese such as Gorgonzola.

1 Preheat the oven to Gas Mark 6/200°C/fan oven 180°C. Place the squash and garlic cloves in a roasting tin, spray with the cooking spray and roast for 25 minutes. Stir the squash, add the whole sage leaves, spray again with the cooking spray, stir and continue cooking for another 10 minutes until the squash is tender and lightly charred.

2 Meanwhile, spray a large non stick frying pan with the cooking spray and heat until hot. Add the rice, stir fry for 1 minute and then add the chopped sage with a ladleful of stock. Let it bubble and be absorbed before adding more, a ladleful at a time. Continue adding the stock, stirring occasionally, until it has all been used and the rice is tender.

3 To serve, set aside the roasted sage leaves, remove the garlic cloves and pop them from their skins. Stir the softened garlic flesh into the risotto together with the squash. Season and warm through over a low heat until piping hot. Add a little water if it becomes too dry. Stir in the Gorgonzola at the last minute and serve garnished with the roasted sage leaves.

Variation... Most blue cheeses will work well here. Try the same amount of Stilton instead of the Gorgonzola.

Seafood risotto

Serves 4
338 calories per serving
Takes 20 minutes to prepare, 50 minutes to cook

850 ml (1½ pints) fish stock
calorie controlled cooking spray
1 fennel bulb, chopped finely
3 shallots, chopped finely
1 garlic clove, crushed
250 g (9 oz) dried Arborio risotto rice
250 g (9 oz) fresh mussels in shells, scrubbed

400 g bag frozen mixed seafood, defrosted
salt and freshly ground black pepper

To serve
1 lemon, quartered
1 tablespoon chopped fresh parsley

Never rinse risotto rice before using it. The starch in the rice helps to create the creamy texture you need for a risotto dish.

1 Gently heat the stock in a large lidded saucepan. Spray a wok or large non stick frying pan with the cooking spray and gently sauté the fennel, shallots and garlic for 5 minutes until softened but not browned.

2 Add the rice to the pan and stir for a couple of minutes until the rice becomes opaque. Add a ladleful of hot stock and stir gently until all the liquid has been absorbed. You'll know the heat of your pan is right if the rice just simmers very gently in the stock. Repeat, stirring after each addition of stock until about a third of the stock is left in the saucepan.

3 Increase the heat of the stock and drop the mussels into the stock saucepan. Cover and cook for 2–3 minutes until the shells open; discard any mussels that remain closed. Remove the mussels with a slotted spoon and set aside in a warm dish. Reduce the stock to a slow simmer again.

continues overleaf ▶

4 Continue adding the remaining stock to the rice a ladleful at a time until all the liquid has been absorbed. If the rice is still a little hard, add a couple of tablespoons of water and continue cooking until it becomes tender and creamy. In total, the cooking time will be approximately 45 minutes.

5 When the rice is nearly ready, stir in the mixed seafood and cook gently for 5 minutes or until the seafood is cooked. Meanwhile, warm four bowls.

6 Season the risotto to taste and serve immediately with the mussels. Arrange the lemon quarters on top and sprinkle with the parsley.

Variation... You can use clams instead of the mussels, but if you don't want to use either, simply omit them.

Bacon and rocket risotto

Serves 6
231 calories per serving
Takes 35 minutes

calorie controlled cooking
  spray
2 onions, sliced
3 garlic cloves, crushed
250 g (9 oz) dried easy cook
  brown rice
4 x 25 g (1 oz) smoked lean
  back bacon rashers, chopped
2 litres (3½ pints) hot chicken
  or vegetable stock
75 g (2¾ oz) low fat soft cheese
  with onion and garlic
110 g (4 oz) rocket
freshly ground black pepper

Adding low fat soft cheese helps create the creamy
consistency normally associated with traditional risotto
rice, but lacking with brown rice.

1 Spray a large non stick frying pan with the cooking spray
and heat until hot. Add the onions, stir fry for 3 minutes
and then add the garlic and continue cooking for another
2 minutes. Add the rice and chopped bacon and stir to coat.

2 Pour in the stock a ladleful at a time, stirring occasionally
and allowing it to be absorbed before adding more. Once all
the stock has been added and the rice is tender, remove from
the heat and stir in the soft cheese. Taste and season with
black pepper. Stir through most of the rocket, reserving a few
leaves for garnish before serving.

Variation... Use the same amount of watercress instead of
the rocket.

Tomato and basil risotto

Serves 2

298 calories per serving

Takes 10 minutes to prepare,
20–25 minutes to cook

calorie controlled cooking
spray

40 g (1½ oz) onion, chopped
finely

1 garlic clove, crushed

100 g (3½ oz) dried Arborio
risotto rice

300 ml (10 fl oz) tomato juice

200 ml (7 fl oz) vegetable stock

1 tablespoon sun-dried tomato
purée

2 ripe tomatoes, peeled,
de-seeded and diced

2 tablespoons virtually fat free
fromage frais

2 tablespoons torn fresh basil
leaves, plus 4 whole leaves,
to garnish

salt and freshly ground black
pepper

*Here is a foolproof recipe for a fresh easy dish to enjoy for
lunch or supper. Serve with a crisp green salad or some
freshly cooked spinach.*

1 Heat a non stick saucepan and spray with the cooking
spray. Add the onion and garlic and cook gently for 5 minutes
or until softened but not coloured. Add the rice and cook for
a further minute, stirring frequently. The rice will become
opaque.

2 In a small saucepan, heat the tomato juice and stock to
simmering point. Add a ladleful of the liquid to the rice and stir
continuously until all the liquid has been used. Repeat, stirring
after each addition, until all the liquid has been absorbed.
The rice will become tender and creamy.

3 Stir in the tomato purée, tomatoes, fromage frais and torn
basil. Season well. Serve immediately garnished with the
whole basil leaves.

Variation... Add 50 g (1¾ oz) of chopped mushrooms with
the last of the tomato juice and sprinkle 1 tablespoon of
freshly grated Parmesan cheese over the risotto.

Lemon and artichoke risotto

Serves 2
326 calories per serving
Takes 40 minutes

**calorie controlled cooking
   spray**
4 spring onions, sliced
2 garlic cloves, sliced
125 g (4½ oz) dried brown rice
**600 ml (20 fl oz) vegetable
   stock**
**grated zest and juice of a small
   lemon**
50 g (1¾ oz) frozen peas
**400 g can artichokes in water,
   drained**
50 g (1¾ oz) low fat soft cheese
**2 tablespoons chopped fresh
   coriander, to garnish**

*Canned artichokes in water are a great store cupboard
standby. Combine them with peas and rice for this lovely
fresh tasting risotto.*

1 Spray a large non stick frying pan with the cooking spray
and heat until hot. Add the spring onions and garlic and stir
fry for 2 minutes until the onions have softened.

2 Add the rice and cook for 1 minute before adding the stock,
a little at a time. Ensure the stock is virtually all absorbed
before adding any more. Continue until all the stock is used
and the rice is tender.

3 Stir in the lemon zest and juice, peas, artichokes and soft
cheese. Warm through to defrost the peas and serve garnished
with the coriander.

Stir fried noodles

Turkey stir fry

Serves 1

447 calories per serving

Takes 15 minutes to prepare,
10 minutes to cook

**40 g (1½ oz) dried thread or
medium egg noodles**

½ a kettleful of boiling water

**2 teaspoons stir fry or
vegetable oil**

**100 g (3½ oz) skinless boneless
turkey breast, cut into strips**

3 spring onions, sliced

**½ red or yellow pepper,
de-seeded and sliced finely**

**1 small carrot, peeled and cut
into thin strips**

2 celery sticks, sliced thinly

1 small garlic clove, crushed

25 g (1 oz) mushrooms, sliced

**a generous pinch of Chinese
five spice**

**1 teaspoon chopped fresh
coriander or chives**

1 teaspoon light soy sauce

1 teaspoon sweet chilli sauce

**salt and freshly ground black
pepper**

**fresh coriander or chives,
chopped, to garnish**

*Quick and colourful, this simple turkey stir fry tastes
superb.*

1 Put the noodles in a bowl and cover with boiling water.
Allow them to soak for 6 minutes or according to the packet
instructions. Drain thoroughly.

2 Meanwhile, heat the oil in a wok or large non stick frying
pan. Add the turkey and stir fry briskly for 4–5 minutes.

3 Add the spring onions, pepper, carrot, celery and garlic. Stir
fry over a high heat for another 3–4 minutes until the turkey
is cooked. The vegetables should remain crisp and crunchy.

4 Add the noodles to the wok or pan along with the mushrooms,
Chinese five spice, coriander or chives, soy sauce and chilli
sauce. Stir fry for 1–2 minutes to heat through thoroughly.

5 Season to taste and serve in a warmed bowl, garnished
with the fresh coriander or chives.

Tip... If you prefer, omit the noodles and serve the stir
fry with 50 g (1¾ oz) of dried long grain rice, cooked
according to the packet instructions.

 Variation... For a vegetarian version, leave out the turkey
and add 100 g (3½ oz) of baby corn and 100 g (3½ oz) of
mange tout or sugar snap peas with the spring onions.

Zanzibar tuna noodles

Serves 4
276 calories per serving
Takes 15 minutes

Kaffir lime leaves give this dish an unmistakeable Thai flavour and are available freeze dried from most large supermarkets in the herb and spice section.

150 g (5½ oz) dried rice noodles

a kettleful of boiling water

1 teaspoon coriander seeds, crushed

½ teaspoon fennel seeds, crushed

calorie controlled cooking spray

1 red onion, chopped finely

a generous pinch of dried chilli flakes

4 freeze dried kaffir lime leaves, crushed

150 g (5½ oz) mange tout

2 x 200 g cans tuna steak in brine, drained

50 g (1¾ oz) mild or hot piquante peppers (e.g. Peppadew), drained and sliced finely

2 tablespoons low fat soft cheese with garlic and herbs

salt and freshly ground black pepper

1 Put the noodles in a bowl and cover with the boiling water. Set aside for 5 minutes.

2 Meanwhile, heat a wok or large non stick frying pan and dry fry the coriander and fennel seeds for 30 seconds. Spray with the cooking spray and add the onion, chilli flakes and lime leaves. Cook gently for 3 minutes, stirring, until the onion begins to soften.

3 Drain the noodles and rinse in cold water. Drain again.

4 Add the mange tout to the wok or pan and stir fry for 2 minutes. Add the tuna, peppers, cheese and 4 tablespoons of water. Stir fry for 1 minute. Take off the heat and fold through the noodles to warm them. Season to taste and serve immediately.

Sweet and sour stir fry

Serves 4
288 calories per serving
Takes 25 minutes

Choose your favourite stir fry vegetables to make this quick and easy supper with its delicious sweet and sour sauce.

3 tablespoons soy sauce
1 tablespoon clear honey
1 tablespoon rice vinegar or white wine vinegar
1 teaspoon chilli sauce
1 teaspoon cornflour
100 g (3½ oz) dried thread egg noodles
a kettleful of boiling water
calorie controlled cooking spray
3 eggs
2 tablespoons skimmed milk
1 tablespoon stir fry oil or sesame oil
1 garlic clove, crushed
1 teaspoon finely grated fresh root ginger
450 g (1 lb) stir fry vegetables, fresh or frozen
25 g (1 oz) cashew nuts
salt and freshly ground black pepper
1 teaspoon sesame seeds, to garnish

1 In a small bowl or jug, mix together the soy sauce, honey, vinegar, chilli sauce and cornflour. Set aside.

2 Put the noodles in a bowl and cover with boiling water. Leave to soak for about 6 minutes or according to the packet instructions. Drain thoroughly.

3 Meanwhile, heat a non stick omelette pan or large non stick frying pan and lightly spray with the cooking spray. Beat the eggs and milk together, pour into the pan and cook until just set. Fold the omelette over, turn it out on to a warm plate and keep warm.

4 Heat the stir fry oil or sesame oil in a wok or large non stick frying pan and add the garlic, ginger and stir fry vegetables. Stir fry briskly for about 3 minutes and then add the hot drained noodles.

5 Stir the soy sauce mixture to blend the ingredients and then add it to the vegetable mixture, tossing to coat everything.

6 Slice the omelette into fine shreds and add it to the pan or wok, stir frying for about 1 minute to reheat it. Add the cashew nuts and seasoning and serve on warmed plates, sprinkled with the sesame seeds.

Variation... For a tasty chicken version, try the recipe on pages 68–9.

Sizzling beef noodles

Serves 4

552 calories per serving

Takes 10 minutes to prepare +
marinating, 15 minutes to cook

**400 g (14 oz) rump steak,
visible fat removed, cut into
thin strips**

For the marinade

2 garlic cloves, crushed

2 tablespoons soy sauce

**2 tablespoons rice wine or dry
sherry**

2 tablespoons honey

For the stir fry

calorie controlled cooking spray

**150 g (5½ oz) broccoli, cut into
florets**

**2 red peppers, de-seeded and
cut into strips**

**8 spring onions, cut diagonally
into 2.5 cm (1 inch) lengths**

4 tablespoons teriyaki sauce

200 g (7 oz) beansprouts

**1 red chilli, de-seeded and cut
into thin strips, or 1 teaspoon
dried chilli flakes**

250 g (9 oz) fresh noodles

**salt and freshly ground black
pepper**

A colourful stir fry bursting with flavour.

1 Mix all the marinade ingredients together in a large bowl
and add the beef. Allow to marinate for as long as possible
up to 2 hours (although 5 minutes will do). Before cooking,
remove the beef from the marinade but reserve the juices.

2 Spray a wok or large non stick frying pan with the cooking
spray, place it over a high heat, add the beef and stir fry for
a few minutes until browned. Remove to a plate and keep
warm.

3 Add the broccoli and 6 tablespoons of water to the wok
or frying pan and stir fry for 5 minutes. Add the peppers and
spring onions and stir fry for a further 3 minutes.

4 Stir in the teriyaki sauce and the reserved marinade.
Return the beef to the pan and add the beansprouts, chilli
and noodles. Stir fry over a high heat for 2 minutes or until
the beef is heated through. Check the seasoning and serve.

Pad Thai

Serves 4

362 calories per serving

Takes 20 minutes + 10 minutes standing

❄

225 g (8 oz) dried thin egg noodles

a kettleful of boiling water

2 tablespoons fish sauce

2 tablespoons tomato purée

1 teaspoon caster sugar

1 teaspoon rice wine vinegar

calorie controlled cooking spray

150 g (5½ oz) white cabbage, shredded

225 g (8 oz) carrots, peeled and grated or cut into thin strips

150 g (5½ oz) beansprouts

6 spring onions, cut into long, thin strips

175 g (6 oz) raw peeled prawns, defrosted if frozen

To serve

25 g (1 oz) salted peanuts, chopped

1 teaspoon chilli flakes

Pad Thai is a traditional noodle dish from Thailand with a fresh, spicy, piquant flavour.

1 Place the noodles in a large bowl and pour boiling water over to just cover them. Leave them to stand for 10 minutes and then drain thoroughly. Mix together the fish sauce, tomato purée, sugar and rice wine vinegar. Set aside.

2 Heat a wok or large non stick frying pan, spray with the cooking spray and add the noodles, cabbage, carrots, beansprouts and spring onions. Stir fry for 5 minutes.

3 Add the prawns and fish sauce mixture to the pan and stir fry for 2–3 minutes until it is all piping hot and the prawns have turned pink and are cooked through.

4 Transfer to four warmed dishes and scatter with the chopped peanuts and chilli flakes to serve.

Sesame noodles with red cabbage

Serves 4
304 calories per serving
Takes 20 minutes

225 g (8 oz) dried medium egg noodles
a kettleful of boiling water
calorie controlled cooking spray
1 red onion, sliced
350 g (12 oz) red cabbage, shredded finely
finely grated zest and juice of an orange
15 g (½ oz) sesame seeds
1 teaspoon sesame oil, to serve

This tasty snack is a wonderful accompaniment to grilled meat or fish.

1 Place the noodles in a large bowl and cover them with boiling water. Leave them to stand for 10 minutes, stirring from time to time. Drain thoroughly.

2 Meanwhile, heat a wok or large non stick frying pan, spray with the cooking spray and add the red onion and cabbage. Stir fry for 5 minutes or until the vegetables begin to soften.

3 Add the noodles to the pan with the orange zest and juice and sesame seeds. Stir fry for a further 2–3 minutes, until everything is piping hot. Drizzle with sesame oil just before serving.

Tip... Sesame oil is strong in flavour, so a little goes a long way. However, it burns even at a low temperature, so it's best used as a flavouring.

Variation... Add 225 g (8 oz) of cubed tofu for a more substantial dish.

Chilli tofu noodles

Serves 2
351 calories per serving
Takes 15 minutes

**calorie controlled cooking
 spray**
150 g (5½ oz) tofu, cubed
**25 g (1 oz) fresh root ginger,
 shredded**
1 tablespoon soy sauce
**2 tablespoons sweet chilli
 sauce**
**30 g (1¼ oz) creamed coconut,
 chopped finely**
juice of a lime
**400 g packet mixed fresh stir
 fry vegetables**
**150 g packet straight to wok
 thick udon noodles**

Bright and zingy, this will tantalise your tastebuds.

1 Heat a wok or non stick frying pan until hot and spray
with the cooking spray. Add the tofu and ginger and cook for
2–3 minutes until starting to brown. Add the soy sauce and
bubble for 30 seconds until almost evaporated. Remove the
tofu and ginger and set aside.

2 In a bowl, mix together the chilli sauce, creamed coconut
and lime juice. Set aside. Heat the wok or pan again and
spray with the cooking spray.

3 Stir fry the vegetables and noodles for 4–5 minutes, stirring
occasionally, and then pour in the chilli mixture and return the
tofu and ginger to the pan. Remove from the heat and keep
stirring constantly until the coconut purée has melted and
everything is coated. Serve immediately.

Sweet and sour chicken

Serves 4
365 calories per serving
Takes 25 minutes

3 tablespoons soy sauce
1 tablespoon clear honey
1 tablespoon rice vinegar or white wine
vinegar
1 teaspoon chilli sauce
1 teaspoon cornflour
100 g (3½ oz) dried thread egg noodles
a kettleful of boiling water
calorie controlled cooking spray
3 eggs

2 tablespoons skimmed milk
1 tablespoon stir fry oil or sesame oil
1 garlic clove, crushed
1 teaspoon finely grated fresh root ginger
450 g (1 lb) stir fry vegetables, fresh or frozen
175 g (6 oz) cooked skinless boneless
chicken breast, chopped
25 g (1 oz) cashew nuts
salt and freshly ground black pepper
1 teaspoon sesame seeds, to garnish

This is a great chicken version of the recipe on page 58.

1 In a small bowl or jug, mix together the soy sauce, honey, vinegar, chilli sauce and cornflour. Set aside.

2 Put the noodles in a bowl and cover with boiling water. Leave to soak for about 6 minutes or according to the packet instructions. Drain thoroughly.

3 Meanwhile, heat a non stick omelette pan or large non stick frying pan and lightly spray with the cooking spray. Beat the eggs and milk together, pour into the pan and cook until just set. Fold the omelette over, turn it out on to a warm plate and keep warm.

4 Heat the stir fry oil or sesame oil in a wok or large non stick frying pan and add the garlic, ginger and stir fry vegetables. Stir fry briskly for about 3 minutes and then add the chicken and hot drained noodles.

5 Stir the soy sauce mixture to blend the ingredients and then add it to the vegetable mixture, tossing to coat everything.

6 Slice the omelette into fine shreds and add it to the pan or wok, stir frying for about 1 minute to reheat it. Add the cashew nuts and seasoning and serve on warmed plates, sprinkled with the sesame seeds.

Tips... You can buy ready prepared fresh or frozen stir fry vegetables – or simply prepare your own. Celery, cucumber, spring onions, Chinese leaves or pak choi, carrots and mushrooms work well together.

If using raw chicken, add to the wok or pan with the garlic and ginger in step 4, cooking for an extra 2–3 minutes before adding the vegetables.

Oyster mushroom noodles

Serves 4
293 calories per serving
Takes 25 minutes
❄

250 g (9 oz) dried medium egg
 noodles
a kettleful of boiling water
calorie controlled cooking
 spray
450 g (1 lb) oyster mushrooms,
 sliced
2 garlic cloves, crushed
6 spring onions, sliced
3 tablespoons oyster sauce
100 ml (3½ fl oz) beef stock
1 teaspoon cornflour
2 tablespoons dry sherry

*This dish is great either on its own or as an
accompaniment to grilled chicken.*

1 Place the noodles in a bowl and cover them with boiling
water. Leave them to stand for 10 minutes, stirring occasionally.

2 Heat a wok or large non stick frying pan, spray with the
cooking spray and stir fry the mushrooms and garlic for
5 minutes, until softened.

3 Drain the noodles and add them to the pan with the spring
onions, oyster sauce and stock. Bring to the boil and cook,
stirring, for 2 minutes.

4 Mix the cornflour to a paste with the sherry and drizzle
this into the pan. Cook, stirring, for 2 minutes until the sauce
thickens. Serve hot.

Tip... Oyster mushrooms are quite delicate, so take care
when stir frying or they may break up.

Ⓥ Variation... For a vegetarian version of this dish, use
soy sauce instead of oyster sauce and vegetable stock
instead of beef.

Vietnamese beef and noodle stir fry

Serves 4
448 calories per serving
Takes 15 minutes

250 g (9 oz) dried rice noodles
calorie controlled cooking spray
400 g (14 oz) lean beef medallion steak, sliced thinly
1 red onion, sliced thinly
2 garlic cloves, sliced
1 red chilli, de-seeded and sliced
250 g (9 oz) beansprouts
juice of ½ a lime
3 tablespoons soy sauce
½ x 25 g packet fresh coriander, sprigs left whole

If you like your food extra hot, leave the seeds in the chilli.

1 Bring a saucepan of water to the boil, add the noodles and cook according to the packet instructions. Drain, rinse in cold water and then drain again.

2 Meanwhile, heat a wok or large non stick frying pan and spray with the cooking spray. Stir fry the sliced steak over a high heat for 3 minutes and then transfer to a plate.

3 Add the onion, garlic and chilli to the pan and stir fry for 2 minutes. Mix in the beansprouts, followed by the noodles, beef, lime juice and soy sauce. Stir fry for 2 minutes until piping hot and well mixed. Mix in the sprigs of coriander just before serving.

Special pork chow mein

Serves 4
326 calories per serving
Takes 40 minutes

400 g (14 oz) lean pork tenderloin
1 tablespoon tandoori spice mix
calorie controlled cooking spray
4 tablespoons dark soy sauce
2 tablespoons rice wine vinegar
2 teaspoons tomato purée
1 garlic clove, crushed
1 red chilli, sliced finely
120 g (4¼ oz) shiitake mushrooms, wiped and sliced
1 carrot, peeled and cut into thin matchsticks
2 small pak choi, leaves separated from the stalks and stalks sliced finely, then both reserved
400 g (14 oz) fresh egg noodles
60 g (2 oz) beansprouts

Look for fresh noodles in the vegetable aisle at the supermarket, beside the packets of stir fry veggies.

1 Preheat the oven to Gas Mark 6/200°C/fan oven 180°C and put a baking tray in to heat.

2 Coat the pork in the tandoori spice mix and spray with the cooking spray. Heat a non stick frying pan until hot and cook the pork for 5 minutes, turning so that each side is brown. Remove the baking tray from the oven, transfer the pork to the tray and cook in the oven for 10–15 minutes until cooked.

3 After 10 minutes, mix together the soy sauce, vinegar and tomato purée in a small jug. Set aside.

4 Heat a wok or non stick frying pan until hot and spray with the cooking spray. Stir fry the garlic and chilli for 1 minute and then add the mushrooms, carrot and pak choi stalks and cook for 5 minutes. Take off the heat.

5 Remove the pork from the oven and cover loosely with foil to keep warm. Set aside.

6 Put the pan or wok back on the heat and add the noodles, beansprouts and pak choi leaves. Stir fry for 3 minutes. Pour in the soy sauce mixture and cook gently for 1 minute, stirring until coated and combined.

7 Divide the noodles between warmed bowls, thinly slice the pork and place on top of the noodles. Serve immediately.

Vegetable chow mein

Serves 4

292 calories per serving

Takes 10 minutes to prepare
+ 10 minutes marinating,
20 minutes to cook

5 teaspoons light soy sauce

1 teaspoon sesame oil

325 g (11½ oz) Quorn Fillet,
cut into strips

150 g (5½ oz) dried medium
egg noodles

calorie controlled cooking
spray

2 garlic cloves, crushed

50 g (1¾ oz) mange tout,
shredded

50 g (1¾ oz) baby corn, halved

3 spring onions, chopped

salt and freshly ground black
pepper

2 tablespoons sesame seeds, to
garnish

Delicious and filling, use any seasonal vegetables for a tasty feast.

1 In a bowl, mix together 2 teaspoons of the soy sauce and the sesame oil. Add the strips of Quorn, stir to coat and leave to marinate for 10 minutes.

2 Bring a saucepan of water to the boil, add the noodles and simmer for 4 minutes or according to the packet instructions. Drain and set aside.

3 Spray a wok or large non stick frying pan with the cooking spray and quickly stir fry the garlic before adding the Quorn strips, marinade, mange tout and baby corn. Stir fry for about 1 minute.

4 Add the noodles, remaining 3 teaspoons of soy sauce and the spring onions. Season and stir fry for 3–4 minutes. Serve, sprinkled with the sesame seeds.

Variation... For a tasty chicken version, see page 82.

Crab and ginger noodles

Serves 2
468 calories per serving
Takes 20 minutes

175 g (6 oz) dried egg noodles
calorie controlled cooking
  spray
1 garlic clove, sliced
200 g (7 oz) pak choi, spring
  greens or spinach, washed
  and sliced
120 g can white crab meat,
  drained
2.5 cm (1 inch) fresh root
  ginger, grated coarsely
3 tablespoons oyster sauce
½ teaspoon dried chilli flakes
100 g (3½ oz) beansprouts

This combination of crab meat, fresh ginger, crunchy beansprouts, hot chilli and noodles is both luxurious and tantalising.

1 Bring a saucepan of water to the boil, add the noodles and cook according to the packet instructions.

2 Meanwhile, heat a wok or large non stick frying pan and spray with the cooking spray. Add the garlic, cook for 1 minute, until turning golden, and then add the green vegetables, crab meat, ginger, oyster sauce, chilli flakes and beansprouts.

3 Stir fry together for a couple of minutes and then serve with the drained noodles.

Spicy lamb stir fry

Serves 2
412 calories per serving
Takes 15 minutes

150 g (5½ oz) lean lamb leg
steak, visible fat removed,
cut into thin strips
300 g bag fresh stir fry
vegetables
1 red chilli, de-seeded and
diced
3 tablespoons light soy sauce
2 x 150 g packets straight to
wok medium noodles

*Make this quick stir fry as spicy as you like by adding
more or less chilli.*

1 Heat a wok or large non stick frying pan until hot. Add the
lamb and dry fry until browned all over.

2 Add the vegetables, chilli and 3 tablespoons of water. Stir
fry for 3–4 minutes until the vegetables are just tender.

3 Add the soy sauce and noodles and heat through. Serve
immediately in warmed bowls.

Tip... Try this recipe with 110 g (4 oz) of raw peeled tiger
prawns instead of the lamb.

Japanese shiitake noodles

Serves 1
304 calories per serving
Takes 15 minutes

calorie controlled cooking
  spray
150 g (5½ oz) shiitake
  mushrooms, halved through
  the stalk
1 small garlic clove, sliced
  finely
1 teaspoon shredded fresh root
  ginger
6 spring onions, cut into thirds
2 tablespoons soy sauce
100 g (3½ oz) pak choi,
  separated into leaves
60 g (2 oz) dried soba noodles
  or medium egg noodles

This Japanese style noodle stir fry can be on the table in 15 minutes or less when you're in need of a speedy but wholesome home cooked meal.

1 Spray a lidded non stick saucepan with the cooking spray, add the mushrooms, garlic, ginger and spring onions and stir fry for 3 minutes until browned.

2 Add the soy sauce and 100 ml (3½ fl oz) of water to the pan, bring to the boil and cook, stirring, for 5 minutes, uncovered, until around 3 tablespoons of syrupy liquid remain. Add the pak choi to the pan, cover and cook for 2 minutes or until the leaves begin to wilt.

3 Meanwhile, bring a saucepan of water to the boil, add the noodles and cook according to the packet instructions. Drain and then toss together with the vegetables. Serve immediately.

Variation... If shiitake mushrooms and pak choi aren't available, substitute chestnut mushrooms and roughly chopped Chinese leaves for a perfectly good alternative.

Chicken chow mein

Serves 4

306 calories per serving

Takes 10 minutes to prepare
+ 10 minutes marinating,
20 minutes to cook

5 teaspoons light soy sauce

1 teaspoon sesame oil

330 g (11½ oz) skinless
  boneless chicken breasts,
  cut into strips

150 g (5½ oz) dried medium
  egg noodles

calorie controlled cooking
  spray

2 garlic cloves, crushed

50 g (1¾ oz) mange tout,
  shredded

50 g (1¾ oz) wafer thin ham,
  shredded

3 spring onions, chopped

salt and freshly ground black
  pepper

2 tablespoons sesame seeds,
  to garnish

*Chow mein literally means 'stir fried noodles' and can
incorporate any meat or vegetable that you wish.*

1 In a bowl, mix together 2 teaspoons of the soy sauce and
the sesame oil. Add the strips of chicken breast, stir to coat
and leave to marinate for 10 minutes.

2 Bring a saucepan of water to the boil, add the noodles and
simmer for 4 minutes or according to the packet instructions.
Drain and set aside.

3 Spray a wok or large non stick frying pan with the cooking
spray. Add the chicken strips and marinade and stir fry for
about 2–3 minutes. Remove to a plate and set aside.

4 Spray the wok or frying pan again with the cooking spray
and quickly stir fry the garlic before adding the mange tout
and ham. Stir fry for about 1 minute.

5 Add the noodles, remaining 3 teaspoons of soy sauce and
the spring onions. Season and stir fry for 2 minutes before
returning the chicken and any juices to the pan. Stir fry for
another 3–4 minutes and serve, sprinkled with the sesame
seeds.

 Variation... For a colourful vegetarian version of this
dish, see page 76.

Rice with spice

Smoked fish kedgeree with oven roasted tomatoes

Serves 4

372 calories per serving

Takes 10 minutes to prepare,
20 minutes to cook

4 tomatoes

4 pinches caster sugar

4 pinches dried thyme or mixed herbs

500 ml (18 fl oz) boiling water

300 g (10½ oz) smoked haddock fillets

250 g (9 oz) dried basmati rice

½ teaspoon salt

2 eggs

3 spring onions, chopped

1 teaspoon mild curry powder

2 teaspoons low fat spread

salt and freshly ground black pepper

Fish and rice makes a filling combination.

1 Preheat the oven to Gas Mark 4/180°C/fan oven 160°C. Halve the tomatoes widthways and place, cut side up, in a shallow dish. Sprinkle with the sugar and herbs and season.

2 Bake the tomatoes for 12–15 minutes, until they are just softened. Remove them from the oven and set aside to cool.

3 Meanwhile, make the kedgeree. Add the boiling water to a frying pan or shallow flameproof pan, add the fish and cook over a gentle heat until the flesh is just firm, this will take about 5 minutes.

4 Pour off the cooking water into a large lidded saucepan. Skin and flake the fish, checking for any bones.

5 Stir the rice into the hot water and add the salt. Bring to the boil, while stirring, reduce the heat, cover and simmer for 10 minutes.

6 Meanwhile, bring a small saucepan of water to the boil, add the eggs and simmer for 8 minutes. Remove from the pan and cool in cold water.

7 When the rice is cooked, mix in the spring onions, curry powder and low fat spread. Stir in the fish and check the seasoning.

8 Peel and quarter the hard boiled eggs. Divide the kedgeree between four warmed plates and top each serving with two egg quarters and two roasted tomato halves.

Chicken tikka lunch box

Serves 4
333 calories per serving
Takes 35 minutes + marinating

225 g (8 oz) skinless boneless chicken breast, diced
100 g (3½ oz) low fat natural yogurt
1 tablespoon tikka curry powder
1 tablespoon fresh lemon juice
1 garlic clove, crushed
225 g (8 oz) dried basmati rice
2 teaspoons sunflower oil
1 red pepper, de-seeded and chopped
1 green pepper, de-seeded and chopped
1 green chilli, de-seeded and chopped finely
1 red onion, chopped
15 g (½ oz) sultanas

You can pack this into a small plastic container and take it to work for a delicious lunch.

1 Mix the chicken with the yogurt, tikka curry powder, lemon juice and garlic. Leave to marinate for 20 minutes.

2 Meanwhile, bring a saucepan of water to the boil, add the rice and cook for about 12 minutes or according to the packet instructions.

3 Heat the oil in a large non stick saucepan, add the chicken and its marinade and stir fry for 10 minutes, until the chicken is cooked through. Add the peppers, chilli and onion and cook for a further 5 minutes.

4 Mix the cooked rice and sultanas into the pan and heat through. Serve hot or allow to cool and then chill in the fridge to serve as a salad.

Variation... Use 225 g (8 oz) of chicken thigh meat instead of chicken breast, if you prefer.

Lamb biryani

Serves 4

365 calories per serving

Takes 28 minutes

175 g (6 oz) dried basmati rice

calorie controlled cooking spray

400 g (14 oz) lean lamb leg steaks, visible fat removed, cubed

½ teaspoon fennel seeds, crushed

1 teaspoon ground coriander

1 teaspoon dried oregano

½ teaspoon turmeric

2 garlic cloves, crushed

3 cardamom pods, split

7 dried curry leaves

100 ml (3½ fl oz) vegetable stock

1 onion, sliced finely

salt and freshly ground black pepper

Biryanis originated in Persia but are now popular in South Asia and other parts of the world.

1 Preheat the oven to Gas Mark 5/190°C/fan oven 170°C. Bring a saucepan of water to the boil, add the rice, bring back to the boil and simmer for 5 minutes.

2 Meanwhile, heat a small, lidded, flameproof and ovenproof casserole dish and spray with the cooking spray. Cook the lamb for 3–4 minutes until browned all over. Stir in the fennel seeds, coriander, oregano, turmeric, garlic, cardamom and curry leaves and season. Keep on a very low heat.

3 Drain the rice and add to the casserole dish along with the vegetable stock. Increase the heat and bring to the boil. Cover tightly and bake in the oven for 10 minutes until the rice is tender.

4 Meanwhile, spray a non stick frying pan with the cooking spray and cook the onion for 6 minutes until golden and crispy. Remove the biryani from the oven and stir to mix through. Serve immediately, topped with the crispy onions.

Balti vegetables and whole spice pilaff

Serves 2

471 calories per serving

Takes 5 minutes to prepare, 25 minutes to cook

1 tablespoon desiccated coconut
300 ml (10 fl oz) boiling water
1 onion, chopped into wedges
1 carrot, peeled and chopped
1 celery stick, sliced thinly
2 teaspoons garlic purée
1 tablespoon ginger purée
1 large green chilli, de-seeded and chopped
2 teaspoons sunflower oil
1–2 teaspoons medium Balti curry powder
2 tablespoons dried red lentils

1 courgette, chopped
2 tablespoons chopped fresh coriander
salt and freshly ground black pepper

For the pilaff

125 g (4½ oz) dried basmati rice
1 bay leaf
½ cinnamon stick
4 whole cardamom pods
¼ teaspoon cumin seeds
¼ teaspoon turmeric

Make your own Balti curry served with an easy cook basmati pilaff, cooked in the traditional way with whole spices that are easy to pick out after cooking and provide all the authentic flavour.

1 In a bowl, cover the desiccated coconut with the boiling water. Set aside for 10 minutes and then strain. Discard the coconut and reserve the liquid.

2 Meanwhile, mix together the onion, carrot, celery, garlic purée, ginger purée, chilli and oil in a large, lidded, non stick saucepan. Heat until the mixture starts to sizzle and then add 3 tablespoons of water. Cover the pan and cook gently for 5 minutes.

3 Remove the lid from the pan, mix in the curry powder and cook briefly. Add the lentils, courgette and reserved coconut water and season.

4 Bring the mixture to the boil, cover and simmer for about 10 minutes. Stir in the coriander and check the seasoning.

5 Meanwhile, make the pilaff. Place the rice in a sieve and rinse it under a cold running tap. Put it in a medium lidded saucepan with 300 ml (10 fl oz) of cold water. Add the bay leaf and spices and season. Bring to the boil, stirring, and then cover and simmer gently for 10 minutes. Do not lift the lid.

6 Allow the rice to stand for 5 minutes and then separate the grains with a fork. Serve the rice with the curry spooned over.

Tips...There are many varieties of basmati rice, choose a good brand for the best fragrance and texture.

The pilaff can be made on its own to serve with other curries or your favourite vegetable stews.

Chicken jalfrezi

Serves 4

318 calories per serving

Takes 10 minutes to prepare,
   25–30 minutes to cook

❄ (up to 1 month)

**calorie controlled cooking
   spray**
1 onion, chopped
2 garlic cloves, crushed
½ teaspoon chilli powder
2 teaspoons curry powder
1 teaspoon tomato purée
**660 g (1 lb 7 oz) skinless
   boneless chicken breasts,
   cut into chunks**
**1 teaspoon grated fresh root
   ginger**
**1 green pepper, de-seeded and
   sliced**
**125 g (4½ oz) dried basmati
   rice**
2 shallots, chopped
½ teaspoon turmeric

*A real must for all curry lovers, this is quite spicy and
absolutely delicious.*

1 Heat a medium non stick frying pan and spray with the
cooking spray. Add the onion and garlic and stir fry for
3–4 minutes until starting to soften. Add a splash of water
if they start to stick.

2 Add the spices and tomato purée and cook for another
minute, stirring to mix well. Add the chicken chunks and
ginger and stir to coat the meat with all the spices.

3 Add the pepper, pour in 150 ml (5 fl oz) of water and bring
to the boil. Simmer for 15–20 minutes until the chicken is
tender.

4 Meanwhile, bring a saucepan of water to the boil, add the
rice and cook according to the packet instructions. Drain.

5 Spray a non stick frying pan with the cooking spray and
cook the shallots for 3–4 minutes until starting to soften.
Stir in the turmeric and mix well.

6 Add the rice and stir to coat with the turmeric. Continue to
stir and cook until all the rice is yellow and hot. Serve with
the chicken.

Variation... Beef or lamb jalfrezi can be cooked in the
same way. Use 600 g (1 lb 5 oz) of lean beef steak or lean
lamb leg steak.

Jungle curry

Serves 6
206 calories per serving
Takes 15 minutes to prepare,
   15 minutes to cook

❄ (up to 1 month)

200 g (7 oz) dried long grain rice
calorie controlled cooking spray
2 garlic cloves, crushed
2 cm (¾ inch) fresh root ginger,
   chopped
1 lemongrass stem, chopped
   finely
1 teaspoon chilli flakes
1 teaspoon curry paste
1 large red onion, chopped
125 g (4½ oz) sugar snap peas
2 red peppers, de-seeded and
   chopped
100 g (3½ oz) baby corn, halved
2 courgettes, sliced
125 g (4½ oz) chestnut
   mushrooms
125 g (4½ oz) green beans,
   trimmed
100 ml (3½ fl oz) vegetable stock
1 tablespoon soy sauce
150 g (5½ oz) fresh spinach,
   washed

A great curry with lots of crunchy vegetables – the perfect spicy vegetarian dish.

1 Bring a saucepan of water to the boil, add the rice and cook according to the packet instructions.

2 Meanwhile, heat a wok or large non stick frying pan and spray with the cooking spray. Stir fry the garlic, ginger and lemongrass for 2–3 minutes before stirring in the chilli flakes and curry paste.

3 Add the red onion, sugar snap peas, red peppers and baby corn and cook for 3–4 minutes, stirring constantly.

4 Add the courgettes, chestnut mushrooms and green beans and then pour in the stock and soy sauce. Bring to the boil and continue to stir fry for a further 4–5 minutes.

5 Finally, add the spinach and stir fry for a further 4–5 minutes until the spinach has wilted and the other vegetables are softening.

6 Serve the curry in warmed bowls with the rice.

Tip... Always cut away the outer leaves of lemongrass and only use the inner ones – the outer leaves are very tough.

Vegetable biryani

Serves 4
256 calories per serving
Takes 30 minutes to prepare,
   30–35 minutes to cook

135 g (5 oz) dried basmati rice
3 tablespoons skimmed milk
2–3 saffron strands
calorie controlled cooking spray
1 large onion, chopped
2 garlic cloves, crushed
1 teaspoon grated fresh root
   ginger
1 teaspoon chilli powder
100 g (3½ oz) broccoli, broken
   into florets
100 g (3½ oz) cauliflower,
   broken into florets
2 courgettes, cut into bite size
   pieces
2 carrots, peeled and chopped
2 red peppers, de-seeded and
   cut into bite size pieces
1 cinnamon stick
2 cardamom pods
½ teaspoon cumin seeds
2 bay leaves
250 g (9 oz) low fat natural yogurt
juice of a lemon

This is a great vegetarian version of the pork recipe on
page 111.

1 Bring a saucepan of water to the boil, add the rice and cook
according to the packet instructions. Drain and set aside.

2 Meanwhile, pour the milk into a jug or bowl and add the
saffron. Leave to infuse for 10–15 minutes. Preheat the oven
to Gas Mark 4/180°C/fan oven 160°C.

3 Heat a medium non stick pan and spray with the cooking
spray. Add the onion and fry until softened and then add the
garlic, ginger and chilli powder and stir.

4 Add all the vegetables and stir fry for 4–5 minutes before
adding the other spices and herbs. Take off the heat and stir
in the yogurt.

5 Layer the rice and the vegetable mixture in an large
ovenproof dish – aim for two layers of each. Add some of
the saffron milk and lemon juice over each layer.

6 Cover and cook for 30–35 minutes until the vegetables
are tender and cooked through.

Spanish tomato rice

Serves 4
432 calories per serving
Takes 40 minutes

calorie controlled cooking spray
1 onion, chopped
2 garlic cloves, crushed
1 red pepper, de-seeded and chopped
1 courgette, chopped
1 teaspoon chilli powder
1 teaspoon turmeric
225 g (8 oz) dried long grain rice
450 ml (16 fl oz) vegetable stock
4 tablespoons dry white wine
400 g can chopped tomatoes
175 g (6 oz) canned black eyed beans, drained and rinsed
90 g (3¼ oz) frozen peas or petit pois
1 tablespoon fresh sage, chopped, or 2 teaspoons dried sage
salt and freshly ground black pepper
60 g (2 oz) Parmesan cheese, grated finely, to serve

This looks great and is delicious eaten hot or cold.

1 Spray a large, lidded, non stick frying pan with the cooking spray, add the onion and garlic and stir fry for 3–4 minutes until softened. Add the pepper and courgette and stir fry for another 2 minutes.

2 Add the chilli, turmeric and rice and stir fry for 2–3 minutes. Add the stock, wine, tomatoes and black eyed beans, bring to the boil, reduce the heat, cover and simmer for 10 minutes.

3 Stir in the peas or petit pois and sage and season. Simmer for another 5 minutes or until the rice is tender. Serve immediately, sprinkled with the Parmesan.

Tip...If the rice becomes dry during cooking, add some more stock or water.

Prawn and tomato curry

Serves 4
550 calories per serving
Takes 35 minutes
❄ (up to 1 month)

400 g can chopped tomatoes
1 onion, diced
1 garlic clove, chopped
4 tablespoons chopped fresh
  coriander
100 g (3½ oz) frozen peas
200 ml (7 fl oz) fish stock
1 teaspoon ground coriander
2 teaspoons ground cumin
2 tablespoons tomato purée
400 g (14 oz) dried brown or
  long grain rice
1.2 litres (2 pints) vegetable
  stock
½ teaspoon turmeric
1 teaspoon ground cumin
500 g (1 lb 2 oz) cooked peeled
  tiger prawns
4 tablespoons low fat fromage
  frais
salt and freshly ground black
  pepper

A warming, spicy curry that is so easy to make.

1 Place the tomatoes, onion, garlic, half the fresh coriander, peas and stock into a saucepan and simmer for 5 minutes.

2 Mix the spices with the tomato purée and add to the tomato mixture in the pan. Simmer for another 5 minutes.

3 Meanwhile, place the rice, stock and spices in a large saucepan, bring to the boil and simmer for 6–8 minutes or until the rice is cooked. Drain.

4 Add the prawns to the tomato mixture and simmer for 2 minutes before stirring in the fromage frais and remaining fresh coriander.

5 Season the curry well and serve with the spicy rice.

One pot spicy chicken and rice

Serves 4

427 calories per serving

Takes 20 minutes to prepare,
20 minutes to cook.

calorie controlled cooking
  spray

340 g (12 oz) skinless boneless
  chicken thighs, diced

1 onion, chopped roughly

1 yellow pepper, de-seeded and
  chopped roughly

1 courgette, chopped roughly

2 garlic cloves, crushed

1 teaspoon paprika

a pinch of chilli flakes

1 teaspoon dried rosemary

175 g (6 oz) dried brown
  basmati rice

230 g can chopped tomatoes

350 ml (12 fl oz) boiling water

410 g can kidney beans,
  drained and rinsed

salt and freshly ground black
  pepper

A simply scrumptious all in one rice dish that is a meal in itself.

1 Heat a large, lidded, non stick, flameproof casserole dish, spray with the cooking spray and brown the chicken for 4–5 minutes over a high heat. Transfer to a plate. Add the onion, pepper and courgette to the casserole and fry for 3 minutes.

2 Stir in the garlic, spices, rosemary and rice, fry for 1 minute and then return the chicken to the casserole with the tomatoes and boiling water.

3 Season well, bring to a simmer and cover. Reduce the heat to a very low setting and cook for 15 minutes.

4 Stir in the kidney beans and cook for a further 5 minutes.

Variation... Replace the chicken thighs with 340 g (12 oz) skinless boneless chicken breasts, cut into chunks.

Mushroom stroganoff with a rice pilaff

Serves 4

299 calories per serving

Takes 10 minutes to prepare, 40 minutes to cook

For the pilaff

1 onion, chopped roughly

1 teaspoon ground cumin

2 teaspoons ground coriander

200 g (7 oz) dried brown lentils

100 g (3½ oz) dried brown basmati rice

1 litre (1¾ pints) vegetable stock

a small bunch of fresh parsley or coriander, to garnish

For the mushrooms

calorie controlled cooking spray

2 garlic cloves, crushed

400 g (14 oz) mushrooms

1 small red chilli, de-seeded and chopped finely

juice of a lemon

100 ml (3½ fl oz) low fat natural yogurt

a small bunch of fresh parsley or thyme, chopped

salt and freshly ground black pepper

This is two recipes in one. The recipes for the pilaff and the stroganoff can be used separately from one another but together they make a very satisfying vegetarian meal.

1 Put all the ingredients for the pilaff, except the garnish, into a large lidded saucepan. Bring to the boil, cover and simmer gently for 35–40 minutes or until the rice is tender and the liquid has been absorbed.

2 Meanwhile, heat a large non stick frying pan, spray with the cooking spray and fry the garlic for 1 minute. Add the mushrooms, stir fry over a high heat for 5 minutes and then add the chilli, lemon juice and seasoning.

3 Cook for a further 2 minutes, turn off the heat, stir the yogurt through and then add the parsley or thyme. Serve with the pilaff, garnished with the parsley or coriander.

Tip... Use large, flat field mushrooms as they are easy to clean and chop and are full of flavour. Chestnut mushrooms are also very good.

Variation... For a special occasion, use the same quantity of wild mushrooms. They are unrivalled for flavour but can be expensive.

Turkey and pepper pilaff

Serves 2
642 calories per serving
Takes 45 minutes
❄

calorie controlled cooking
    spray
225 g (8 oz) skinless boneless
    turkey breast, sliced, or
    turkey stir fry strips
2 spring onions, chopped
1 carrot, peeled and grated
1 green or yellow pepper,
    de-seeded and sliced
175 g (6 oz) dried easy cook
    long grain rice
1–2 teaspoons mild curry
    powder
600 ml (20 fl oz) chicken stock
1 tablespoon light soy sauce
2 tablespoons chopped fresh
    parsley
salt and freshly ground black
    pepper

To serve
15 g (½ oz) flaked almonds
2 tablespoons low fat natural
    yogurt

This is vibrant and quick and a delicious meal.

1 Heat a large, lidded, heavy based frying pan until quite
hot and spray with the cooking spray. Stir fry the turkey for
2 minutes until browned and then remove from the pan with
a slotted spoon.

2 Spray the pan with the cooking spray again and stir fry the
spring onions, carrot and pepper for 2 minutes. Add the rice
and curry powder and cook for a further minute.

3 Pour in the stock and soy sauce, return the turkey to the
pan and bring it all to the boil, stirring continuously. Cover
the pan, turn down the heat to a gentle simmer and cook for
15 minutes.

4 Meanwhile, heat a small non stick frying pan, add the
flaked almonds and toast until golden. Be careful not to let
them burn. Set aside.

5 Check the seasoning of the pilaff and cook for a further
3–5 minutes until all the liquid has been absorbed.

6 Stir in the parsley and serve on warm plates topped with a
tablespoon of yogurt and sprinkled with the toasted almonds.

Tip... You can buy toasted flaked almonds in most major
supermarkets.

Variation... For a stunning vegetarian version, see the
recipe on page 116.

Pork biryani

Serves 4

290 calories per serving

Takes 25 minutes to prepare,
40–45 minutes to cook

135 g (4¾ oz) dried basmati
 rice
3 tablespoons skimmed milk
2–3 saffron strands
calorie controlled cooking
 spray
1 large onion, chopped
2 garlic cloves, crushed
1 teaspoon grated fresh root
 ginger
1 teaspoon chilli powder
325 g (11½ oz) pork tenderloin,
 cut into bite size pieces
1 cinnamon stick
2 cardamom pods
½ teaspoon cumin seeds
2 bay leaves
250 g (9 oz) low fat natural
 yogurt
juice of a lemon

*A biryani is a great one pot meal. Serve with a crunchy
vegetable, such as broccoli or braised celery.*

1 Bring a saucepan of water to the boil, add the rice and
cook according to the packet instructions. Drain and set aside.

2 Meanwhile, pour the milk into a jug or bowl and add the
saffron. Leave to infuse for 10–15 minutes. Preheat the oven
to Gas Mark 4/180°C/fan oven 160°C.

3 Heat a medium non stick pan and spray with the cooking
spray. Add the onion and fry until softened and then add the
garlic, ginger and chilli powder and stir.

4 Add the pork and stir fry for 4–5 minutes, browning on all
sides, before adding the other spices and herbs. Take off the
heat and stir in the yogurt.

5 Layer the rice and the pork mixture in an large ovenproof
dish – aim for two layers of each. Add some of the saffron
milk and lemon juice over each layer.

6 Cover and cook for 40–45 minutes until the pork is tender
and cooked through.

♥ Variation... For a fantastic vegetarian version, see the
recipe on page 98.

Vegetable chilli

Serves 4
368 calories per serving
Takes 15 minutes to prepare,
  30 minutes to cook

calorie controlled cooking
  spray
1 large onion, chopped
2 garlic cloves, crushed
3 celery sticks, chopped finely
1 large carrot, peeled and
  chopped finely
1 courgette, chopped
350 g packet Quorn mince
2–3 teaspoons chilli powder
400 g can chopped tomatoes
2 tablespoons tomato purée
215 g can red kidney beans,
  drained and rinsed
198 g can sweetcorn with
  peppers, drained
300 ml (10 fl oz) hot vegetable
  stock
175 g (6 oz) dried long grain
  rice
salt and freshly ground black
  pepper

*Bring the flavours of Mexico to your table with this
easy-to-make tasty vegetarian chilli.*

1 Heat a large, lidded, non stick saucepan and spray with
the cooking spray. Add the onion, garlic, celery, carrot and
courgette. Stir fry for 2–3 minutes.

2 Add the Quorn mince, chilli powder, tomatoes, tomato
purée, kidney beans, sweetcorn with peppers and stock.
Stir well and bring to the boil. Cover, reduce the heat and
simmer for about 30 minutes, stirring from time to time.

3 Around 15 minutes before you are ready to serve, bring
a saucepan of water to the boil, add the rice and cook for
about 12 minutes until tender, or according to the packet
instructions. Drain thoroughly.

4 Check the flavour of the chilli and season according to
taste. Divide the cooked rice between four warmed serving
plates and pile the chilli on top. Serve at once.

Tips...Cook spicy food according to your taste, adding
extra chilli powder if you like things spicy, or use it
sparingly if you prefer a milder flavour.

Cans of sweetcorn with peppers are available in
supermarkets. Although not as quick, you could also
use 150 g (5½ oz) of sweetcorn and 50 g (1¾ oz) of
chopped peppers.

Chicken tikka masala

Serves 4

358 calories per serving

Takes 15 minutes to prepare
+ at least 1 hour marinating,
25 minutes to cook

❄

**2 tablespoons tikka masala
curry paste**

**150 g (5½ oz) 0% fat Greek
yogurt**

**450 g (1 lb) skinless boneless
chicken breasts, cut into
chunks**

calorie controlled cooking spray

1 red onion, sliced thinly

**1 teaspoon grated fresh root
ginger or 1 teaspoon ready
prepared 'fresh' ginger**

400 g can chopped tomatoes

150 ml (5 fl oz) chicken stock

**2 tablespoons chopped fresh
coriander**

100 g (3½ oz) dried basmati rice

**salt and freshly ground black
pepper**

To garnish

**5 cm (2 inch) cucumber,
chopped finely**

a few fresh coriander sprigs

*This colourful creamy dish is one of the nation's
favourites.*

1 Put the curry paste into a non-metallic bowl and mix in
90 g (3¼ oz) of the yogurt, reserving the rest for later. Add the
chicken, stir well and then cover and leave to marinate in the
fridge for at least 1 hour or overnight.

2 When ready to cook, heat a large non stick saucepan and
spray with the cooking spray. Add most of the onion, reserving
some to garnish. Sauté for 1–2 minutes and then add the
ginger and marinated chicken mixture. Cook for 2–3 minutes.

3 Add the tomatoes, stock and chopped coriander to the
saucepan. Bring up to the boil, reduce the heat and simmer,
uncovered, over a low heat for 20–25 minutes. Season to
taste.

4 When the chicken has simmered for 10 minutes, bring
a saucepan of water to the boil, add the rice and cook
according to the packet instructions.

5 Serve the rice with the cooked chicken, garnished with
the reserved yogurt, remaining red onion, cucumber and
coriander sprigs.

❂ **Variation...** For a fantastic vegetarian version of this
dish, see page 122.

Vegetable pilaff

Serves 2
725 calories per serving
Takes 40 minutes

calorie controlled cooking
  spray
2 spring onions, chopped
1 carrot, peeled and grated
**1 green or yellow pepper,
  de-seeded and sliced**
**175 g (6 oz) dried easy cook
  long grain rice**
**1–2 teaspoons mild curry
  powder**
**600 ml (20 fl oz) vegetable
  stock**
1 tablespoon light soy sauce
**350 g (12 oz) canned drained
  chick peas**
**2 tablespoons chopped fresh
  parsley**
**salt and freshly ground black
  pepper**

To serve
**15 g (½ oz) toasted flaked
  almonds**
**2 tablespoons low fat natural
  yogurt**

*This is a wonderful vegetarian version of the recipe on
page 108.*

1 Heat a large, lidded, heavy based frying pan until quite hot
and spray with the cooking spray. Stir fry the spring onions,
carrot and pepper for 2 minutes. Add the rice and curry
powder and cook for a further minute.

2 Pour in the stock, soy sauce and chick peas and bring it all
to the boil, stirring continuously. Cover the pan, turn down the
heat to a gentle simmer and cook for 15 minutes.

3 Check the seasoning of the pilaff and cook for a further
3–5 minutes until all the liquid has been absorbed.

4 Stir in the parsley and serve on warmed plates topped
with a tablespoon of yogurt and sprinkled with the toasted
almonds.

Tip... If you can't find toasted flaked almonds, heat a small
non stick frying pan, add 15 g (½ oz) of flaked almonds
and toast until golden. Be careful not to let them burn.

Thai coconut cod with fruited pilau rice

Serves 2

442 calories per serving

Takes 10 minutes to prepare,
20 minutes to cook

1 tablespoon cornflour

2 tablespoons dry sherry

1 tablespoon half fat crème fraîche

1 teaspoon green or red curry paste

1 garlic clove, crushed

¼ teaspoon coconut essence

2 x 150 g (5½ oz) cod fillets

salt and freshly ground black pepper

For the rice

50 g (1¾ oz) dried basmati rice

1 tablespoon flaked almonds

1 carrot, peeled and grated

2 spring onions, sliced

2 pieces stem ginger in syrup, chopped finely

1 tablespoon sultanas

a small bunch of fresh parsley, chopped

1 teaspoon ground coriander

This recipe uses coconut essence, available in the bakery sections of large supermarkets, instead of creamed coconut, for a healthier alternative without losing any of the coconut flavour.

1 Preheat the oven to Gas Mark 4/180°C/fan oven 160°C. Line a baking sheet with a large piece of foil – enough to make a parcel for the fish.

2 Mix the cornflour with the sherry to make a smooth paste. Add the crème fraîche, curry paste, garlic and coconut essence.

3 Season the cod and place in the foil. Pour over the crème fraîche mixture and seal up the edges to make a parcel. Bake in the oven for 20 minutes.

4 Meanwhile, bring a saucepan of water to the boil, add the rice and cook according to the packet instructions. Drain well. Heat a small non stick frying pan, add the flaked almonds and toast until golden. Be careful not to let them burn.

5 Add all the remaining ingredients to the rice, including the almonds, season and toss together. Divide the rice between two plates and serve with the cod and its sauce.

Variation... Try this recipe using 300 g (10½ oz) of raw peeled prawns instead of the cod, adding to the parcel in step 3.

Vegetable pilau

Serves 2
451 calories per serving
Takes 50 minutes

150 g (5½ oz) dried brown
basmati rice
600 ml (20 fl oz) vegetable stock
2 eggs
60 g (2 oz) fine green beans,
trimmed and sliced
1 carrot, peeled and diced
1 baby cauliflower, cut into
small florets
calorie controlled cooking spray
1 onion, chopped
1 teaspoon coriander seeds,
crushed
1 teaspoon cumin seeds,
crushed
2 teaspoons garam masala
1 teaspoon turmeric
75 g (2¾ oz) mushrooms, sliced
2 garlic cloves, chopped
2.5 cm (1 inch) fresh root
ginger, chopped finely
1 tablespoon tomato purée
salt and freshly ground black
pepper

A spicy rice dish for a special supper.

1 Put the rice into a medium lidded saucepan and cover with the stock. Bring to the boil, reduce the heat to its lowest setting, cover and simmer for 30 minutes or until tender.

2 Meanwhile, bring a small saucepan of water to the boil, add the eggs and simmer for 8 minutes. Remove from the pan and cool in cold water. Peel and halve.

3 Bring a lidded saucepan of water to the boil, put the beans, carrot and cauliflower in a steamer basket and place it over the pan. Cover and cook until just tender but not completely cooked. Alternatively, bring a small amount of water to the boil and cook the vegetables for 5 minutes. Refresh the vegetables under cold running water and leave to drain.

4 Remove the rice from the heat and set aside, still covered, for 5 minutes. Drain if necessary, but all the stock should have been absorbed by the rice.

5 Heat a non stick frying pan and spray with the cooking spray. Fry the onion for 7 minutes and then add the coriander and cumin seeds and cook for 1 minute.

6 Spray the pan again with the cooking spray and stir in the ground spices, mushrooms, garlic and ginger. Cook for 2 minutes and then stir in the tomato purée and 150 ml (5 fl oz) of water. Continue cooking and stirring over a medium-low heat for 5 minutes.

7 Add the rice and vegetables, mix together, season and heat through, stirring gently. Serve, topping each serving with two egg halves.

Snappy jambalaya

Serves 4

427 calories per serving

Takes 10 minutes to prepare,
   20 minutes to cook

❄ (without the fish)

**calorie controlled cooking
   spray**

2 large onions, chopped

1 celery stick, chopped

**1 red pepper, de-seeded and
   diced**

**225 g (8 oz) button mushrooms,
   sliced**

100 g (3½ oz) lean ham, diced

400 g can chopped tomatoes

2 bay leaves

2 garlic cloves, crushed

**1 red chilli, de-seeded and
   chopped finely, or ½ teaspoon
   dried chilli flakes**

**225 g (8 oz) dried long grain
   rice**

700 ml (1¼ pints) chicken stock

**4 x 125 g (4½ oz) red snapper
   fillets**

**salt and freshly ground black
   pepper**

**a small bunch of fresh parsley,
   chopped, to garnish**

*A great big fish and rice dish with bold flavours from the
American Deep South.*

1 Heat a large non stick frying pan, spray with the cooking
spray and fry the onions for 4 minutes until softened. Add the
celery, pepper and mushrooms and stir fry for 10 minutes.

2 Add the ham, tomatoes, bay leaves, garlic, chilli and
150 ml (5 fl oz) of water. Season, stir together and then
simmer for 15 minutes.

3 Add the rice and stock and simmer gently for 20 minutes,
stirring every now and then, until the rice is just cooked and
the sauce is almost completely absorbed.

4 Meanwhile, preheat the grill to medium-high. Season the
snapper fillets and grill for 2–3 minutes or until golden and
cooked through.

5 Spoon the jambalaya on to serving plates or into big wide
bowls, top each with a snapper fillet and sprinkle with the
parsley.

Quorn tikka masala

Serves 4

342 calories per serving

Takes 15 minutes to prepare
+ at least 1 hour marinating,
10–15 minutes to cook

2 tablespoons tikka masala
  curry paste

150 g (5½ oz) 0% fat Greek
  yogurt

450 g (1 lb) Quorn Chicken Style
  Pieces

calorie controlled cooking
  spray

1 red onion, sliced thinly

1 teaspoon grated fresh root
  ginger

400 g can chopped tomatoes

150 ml (5 fl oz) vegetable stock

2 tablespoons chopped fresh
  coriander

100 g (3½ oz) dried basmati
  rice

salt and freshly ground black
  pepper

To garnish

5 cm (2 inch) cucumber,
  chopped finely

a few sprigs of fresh coriander

*This is a fabulous vegetarian version of the recipe on
page 114.*

1 Put the curry paste into a non-metallic bowl and mix in
90 g (3¼ oz) of the yogurt, reserving the rest for later. Add
the Quorn, stir well and then cover and leave to marinate in
the fridge for at least 1 hour or overnight.

2 When ready to cook, heat a large non stick saucepan and
spray with the cooking spray. Add most of the onion, reserving
some to garnish. Sauté for 1–2 minutes and then add the
ginger and marinated Quorn mixture. Cook for 2–3 minutes.

3 Add the tomatoes, stock and chopped coriander to the
saucepan. Bring up to the boil, reduce the heat and simmer,
uncovered, over a low heat for 10–15 minutes. Season to
taste.

4 Meanwhile, bring a saucepan of water to the boil, add the
rice and cook according to the packet instructions.

5 Serve the rice with the Quorn masala, garnished with
the reserved yogurt, remaining red onion, cucumber and
coriander sprigs.

Prawn pilaff

Serves 4

325 calories per serving

Takes 15 minutes to prepare,
  35 minutes to cook

**calorie controlled cooking
  spray**

2 onions, sliced thinly

**2 green chillies, de-seeded and
  diced**

1 teaspoon garam masala

1 teaspoon turmeric

juice of a lemon

225 g (8 oz) dried brown rice

**1 litre (1¾ pints) vegetable
  stock**

**225 g (8 oz) cooked peeled
  prawns, defrosted if frozen**

110 g (4 oz) frozen peas

**4 tablespoons chopped fresh
  coriander, to garnish**

*A pilaff is a spiced rice dish that usually has meat or
vegetables, but this version uses prawns.*

1 Heat a large, lidded, non stick frying pan and spray with
the cooking spray. Add the onions and stir fry for 5 minutes
until soft.

2 Add the chillies, spices, lemon juice and rice. Cook, stirring,
for 1 minute.

3 Add the stock and bring to the boil. Cover and cook for
30 minutes until the rice is tender and most of the stock
has been absorbed.

4 Stir in the prawns and peas and cook for a further 5 minutes
until heated through. Serve garnished with the coriander.

Moroccan spiced rice with lamb

Serves 4
454 calories per serving
Takes 30 minutes to prepare,
  20 minutes to cook

350 g (12 oz) lean lamb mince
1 onion, sliced
2 garlic cloves, crushed
½ teaspoon ground ginger
½ teaspoon ground cinnamon
1 teaspoon paprika
1 aubergine, diced
225 g (8 oz) courgettes, diced
225 g (8 oz) dried long grain
  rice
400 ml (14 fl oz) lamb stock
450 g (1 lb) plum tomatoes,
  skinned, de-seeded and diced
2 tablespoons chopped fresh
  mint, plus a few extra leaves,
  to garnish

With the authentic combination of ginger, cinnamon and mint, this Moroccan dish is absolutely delicious.

1 Heat a heavy based non stick frying pan and add the lamb mince. Dry fry for 5 minutes, draining off any excess fat. Add the onion, garlic, ginger, cinnamon and paprika and stir well.

2 Add the aubergine, courgettes, rice and stock and bring to the boil. Cover and simmer for 20 minutes until the stock has been absorbed and the rice is tender.

3 Add the tomatoes and mint and heat through. Spoon the mixture into a warmed serving dish and scatter with a few extra mint leaves.

Tip... The easiest way to skin tomatoes is to plunge them into boiling water for a few seconds – the skins will then peel off easily.

Cashew and watercress pilau

Serves 1

501 calories per serving

Takes 20 minutes to prepare,
 35 minutes to cook

**calorie controlled cooking
 spray**

3 spring onions, chopped

1 garlic clove, chopped

**75 g (2¾ oz) dried brown
 basmati rice**

**¼ cauliflower, chopped into
 small florets**

juice of ½ a lemon

¼ teaspoon Chinese five spice

**100 ml (3½ fl oz) vegetable
 stock**

**a small bunch of fresh mint,
 chopped**

**a small bunch of fresh parsley,
 chopped**

25 g (1 oz) cashew nuts

**100 g (3½ oz) watercress,
 chopped**

**salt and freshly ground black
 pepper**

A satisfying and comforting meal.

1 Heat a large, lidded, non stick pan and spray with the cooking spray. Stir fry the spring onions and garlic for a few minutes, adding a splash of water if they start to stick.

2 Add all the other ingredients except the cashew nuts and watercress and stir together. Cover the pan and simmer for 35 minutes without lifting the lid.

3 Meanwhile, toast the cashew nuts in a dry non stick frying pan until golden (be careful not to let them burn). Set aside to cool and then chop.

4 Stir the cashew nuts and watercress into the pilau, season and serve.

Paella

Serves 4

478 calories per serving

Takes 10 minutes to prepare,
35 minutes to cook

calorie controlled cooking
spray

**300 g (10½ oz) skinless
boneless chicken breasts,
cut into bite size pieces**

1 onion, chopped

**1 red pepper, de-seeded and
chopped**

3 garlic cloves, crushed

3 ripe tomatoes, chopped

a generous pinch of saffron

2 teaspoons paprika

**a small bunch of fresh thyme,
woody stems removed and
leaves chopped**

**250 g (9 oz) dried brown or long
grain rice**

**1.2 litres (2 pints) chicken
stock**

**400 g (14 oz) frozen seafood,
defrosted if frozen**

125 g (4½ oz) frozen peas

**salt and freshly ground black
pepper**

lemon wedges, to serve

*Rice and saffron are the only really essential ingredients
in this dish, so there's lots of room for creativity.*

1 Spray a large non stick pan with the cooking spray, add the
chicken and sauté for 5 minutes, stirring frequently. Season,
remove from the pan to a plate and set aside.

2 Spray the pan again with the cooking spray, add the onion,
red pepper and garlic and stir fry for 4 minutes or until softened.
Add the tomatoes, saffron, paprika and thyme and cook for a
further 2 minutes.

3 Add the rice, stir until well mixed and then add half the
stock. Bring to a simmer and cook for 10 minutes. Add the
rest of the stock, return the chicken to the pan and cook for
a further 10 minutes without stirring. Lastly, add the seafood
and the peas. Stir once, gently, and cook for 5 minutes or
until the rice is tender.

4 Check the seasoning and serve with lemon wedges to
squeeze over.

Simply special

Sweet and sour prawns

Serves 4
196 calories per serving
Takes 20 minutes to prepare,
  10 minutes to cook

110 g (4 oz) dried basmati rice
calorie controlled cooking
  spray
2 garlic cloves, sliced
2 cm (¾ inch) fresh root ginger,
  chopped
5 spring onions, chopped into
  long pieces
1 red pepper, de-seeded and cut
  into square pieces
250 g (9 oz) raw peeled tiger
  prawns
200 g can water chestnuts,
  drained

For the sauce
1 teaspoon cornflour
100 ml (3½ fl oz) fish stock
3 tablespoons soy sauce
1 tablespoon rice vinegar
1 tablespoon tomato purée
2 teaspoons artificial sweetener

A delicious, healthier version of this popular Chinese dish.

1 Bring a saucepan of water to the boil, add the rice and cook according to the packet instructions. Drain.

2 Meanwhile, heat a wok or large non stick frying pan and spray with the cooking spray. Add the garlic, ginger, spring onions and red pepper and stir fry for 4–5 minutes.

3 Add the prawns and water chestnuts and cook for 1 minute.

4 In a jug, mix the cornflour to a paste with 3 teaspoons of water. Add all the other sauce ingredients, mix together and pour into the wok or frying pan. Stir fry for 3–4 minutes until the sauce starts to thicken. Serve the prawns with the basmati rice.

Tip... Water chestnuts are a sweet, crunchy bulb about the size of a walnut and are sold in most supermarkets and Chinese grocers.

Beef red curry

Serves 4
332 calories per serving
Takes 20 minutes

calorie controlled cooking
  spray
300 g (10½ oz) lean rump steak,
  cut into pieces
2 tablespoons red Thai curry
  paste
1 green pepper, de-seeded and
  sliced
150 g (5½ oz) baby corn
½ x 400 ml can reduced fat
  coconut milk
300 ml (10 fl oz) vegetable
  stock
110 g (4 oz) beansprouts
2 x 150 g packets straight to
  wok Udon noodles
a handful of chopped fresh
  coriander, to garnish

Red Thai curry paste tends to be hotter than green, so be careful how much you use.

1 Heat a large, lidded, non stick saucepan until hot. Spray with the cooking spray and add the steak. Stir fry for 2–3 minutes until brown.

2 Add the curry paste, pepper and baby corn. Cook for a further 2–3 minutes until beginning to brown.

3 Add the coconut milk and stock. Bring to the boil, cover and simmer for 10 minutes until the beef is tender.

4 Add the beansprouts and noodles. Cook for 1–2 minutes until hot and then serve in warmed bowls garnished with the coriander.

Variation... For a wonderful seafood version, see the recipe on page 156.

Grilled salmon with stir fry veg

Serves 2

569 calories per serving

Takes 10 minutes to prepare,
35 minutes to cook

120 g (4¼ oz) dried brown rice

2.5 cm (1 inch) fresh root
  ginger, grated finely

1 garlic clove, crushed

4 tablespoons soy sauce

2 x 150 g (5½ oz) salmon fillets

calorie controlled cooking
  spray

4 spring onions, sliced

200 g (7 oz) cabbage, shredded

200 g (7 oz) cauliflower, cut into
  small florets

100 ml (3½ fl oz) vegetable
  stock

A tasty dish that is perfect for autumn or winter.

1 Bring a saucepan of water to the boil, add the rice and cook according to the packet instructions.

2 Meanwhile, in a small bowl, mix together the ginger, garlic and 2 tablespoons of the soy sauce. Place the salmon fillets on a plate and pour over the sauce. Place in the fridge.

3 Spray a large non stick frying pan or wok with the cooking spray and place on a high heat. Toss all the vegetables together in the pan or wok until browned on the edges, about 3–4 minutes.

4 Add the stock and remaining soy sauce and stir fry for a few more minutes. Keep warm while you cook the salmon.

5 Remove the salmon from the fridge and place on a grill pan. Preheat the grill to medium. Scrape any remaining ginger, garlic and soy from the plate into the pan or wok and stir into the vegetables. Cook the salmon under the grill for 3–4 minutes on each side, or until just cooked through.

6 Drain the rice and serve it with the salmon on a bed of stir fry vegetables.

Variation... If you like chillies, try adding a fresh chopped chilli to the stir fried vegetables.

Meatballs with Moroccan rice

Serves 6

435 calories per serving

Takes 30 minutes to prepare,
   45 minutes to cook

a large pinch of saffron

2 tablespoons boiling water

calorie controlled cooking spray

2 onions, diced

3 garlic cloves, crushed

600 g (1 lb 5 oz) lean beef
   mince

1 tablespoon dried mixed herbs

325 g (11½ oz) dried basmati
   rice

3 carrots, peeled and chopped

3 cardamom pods

2 teaspoons coriander seeds,
   crushed lightly

2 teaspoons cumin seeds,
   crushed lightly

1 cinnamon stick

2 bay leaves

finely grated zest and juice of
   1½ lemons

40 g (1½ oz) ready to eat dried
   apricots, chopped

1.5 litres (2¾ pints) vegetable
   stock

salt and freshly ground black
   pepper

Impress friends and family with this unusual dish.

1 Place the saffron in a small bowl and cover with the boiling water. Set aside to infuse.

2 Spray a large non stick frying pan with the cooking spray and heat. Add the onions and stir fry for 3–4 minutes until soft. Add the garlic and cook for another 2 minutes. Remove from the heat.

3 Place the mince in a large bowl and mix in 3 tablespoons of the onion mixture and the herbs. Season. Using wet hands, shape the mixture into 18 meatballs. Spray the frying pan again with the cooking spray and heat until hot. Cook the meatballs, turning frequently, for 10 minutes until browned. Set aside.

4 Place all the remaining ingredients, including the saffron and its liquid and the remaining onion mixture, into a large lidded saucepan. Cover, bring to the boil and simmer for 30 minutes.

5 Add the meatballs and continue cooking for 10–15 minutes until the rice is tender. To serve, divide the rice between warmed plates and top with the meatballs.

Braised Chinese vegetables

Serves 2
204 calories per serving
Takes 20 minutes

calorie controlled cooking spray
1 garlic clove, chopped
2.5 cm (1 inch) fresh root ginger, cut into very thin matchsticks
200 g (7 oz) pak choi
6 spring onions, chopped into short lengths
100 g (3½ oz) baby corn
200 ml (7 fl oz) vegetable stock
1 tablespoon light soy sauce
225 g (8 oz) mixed Oriental mushrooms, halved if large
75 g (2¾ oz) dried rice noodles
a kettleful of boiling water

Full of flavour, this is a wonderfully soothing meal for autumn nights.

1 Heat a wok or lidded non stick frying pan and spray with the cooking spray. Add the garlic and ginger and stir fry for 1 minute.

2 Cut the pak choi in half where the green leaves join the whiter stem. Slice any large white parts into two and add the stems to the wok with the spring onions, baby corn, stock, soy sauce and mushrooms. Bring to a simmer, cover and braise for 6 minutes, stirring occasionally.

3 Meanwhile, place the noodles in a bowl and cover them with boiling water. Leave them to stand for 3 minutes or according to the packet instructions. Drain and put into two warmed shallow bowls.

4 Finally, add the green pak choi leaves to the wok. Increase the heat, replace the lid and allow them to wilt in the hot liquid for a minute or two. Place the vegetables on top of the noodles and serve straight away.

Porcupine meatballs in red wine sauce

Serves 6

252 calories per serving

Takes 30 minutes to prepare,
30 minutes to cook

*These meatballs, made with rice, are inspired by a New
Zealand dish. The rice puffs up as it cooks and sticks out
of the meatballs giving them a spiky appearance, hence
the name.*

calorie controlled cooking
spray

1 onion, chopped finely

2 garlic cloves, crushed

400 g (14 oz) extra lean beef
mince

150 g (5½ oz) dried long grain
rice

a small bunch of fresh thyme,
woody stems removed and
leaves chopped, plus extra to
garnish

2 carrots, peeled and diced
finely

100 ml (3½ fl oz) red wine

400 g can chopped tomatoes

1 tablespoon Worcestershire
sauce

300 ml (10 fl oz) vegetable
stock

salt and freshly ground black
pepper

1 Heat a large, lidded, non stick frying pan, spray with the
cooking spray and stir fry the onion and garlic for 5 minutes,
or until softened, adding a splash of water if they start to stick.

2 Take off the heat and place the onion and garlic in a large
bowl with the beef mince, rice, thyme and carrots. Season.
Using wet hands, mix together well and then roll into 30 ping
pong sized balls, squashing the mixture together with your
hands.

3 In the same frying pan, brown the meatballs on all sides.
Add all the remaining ingredients, bring to the boil and then
cover and simmer for 30 minutes on a low heat. Serve
garnished with the reserved thyme.

Tofu fried rice

Serves 2
381 calories per serving
Takes 20 minutes

100 g (3½ oz) dried long grain rice
calorie controlled cooking spray
6 spring onions, chopped
1 red pepper, de-seeded and diced
1 garlic clove, crushed
60 g (2 oz) canned sweetcorn, drained
75 g (2¾ oz) fresh or frozen peas
125 g (4½ oz) smoked tofu, cut into chunks
1 egg, beaten
1 tablespoon soy sauce

Bright and colourful, this is a great vegetarian version of the recipe on page 168.

1 Bring a saucepan of water to the boil, add the rice and cook for 15 minutes or according to the packet instructions. Drain.

2 After about 10 minutes, heat a wok or non stick frying pan and spray with the cooking spray. Add the spring onions, red pepper and garlic and stir fry for 2 minutes.

3 Add the sweetcorn, peas, tofu and cooked rice. Stir fry for a further minute.

4 Make a space in the bottom of the wok among the vegetables and pour in some of the egg. Stir it so that it sets in little pieces and then repeat this pouring and stirring with the rest of the egg.

5 Mix everything together and serve immediately with a little soy sauce to taste.

Chilli noodle crab nests

Serves 6
239 calories per serving
Takes 25 minutes
❄ (cooked crab nests only)

2 x 170 g cans white crab meat,
  drained
2 eggs, beaten
2 tablespoons tikka masala
  curry paste
2 tablespoons chopped fresh
  coriander
350 g (12 oz) fresh egg noodles
calorie controlled cooking
  spray

For the coleslaw
4 tablespoons reduced fat
  mayonnaise
grated zest and juice of a lime
1 large carrot, peeled and
  grated
200 g (7 oz) beansprouts
½ red chilli, de-seeded and
  chopped finely
salt and freshly ground black
  pepper

Serve with 1 tablespoon of mango chutney, 20 g (¾ oz) of prawn crackers per person and a mixed salad.

1 Preheat the oven to Gas Mark 6/200°C/fan oven 180°C. In a large bowl, mix together the crab meat, eggs, curry paste and coriander. Add the noodles and mix gently to combine.

2 Spray a 12 hole non stick muffin tin with the cooking spray and divide the mixture between the holes. Cook in the oven for 15 minutes until set.

3 Meanwhile, to make the coleslaw, in another bowl mix together the mayonnaise and lime zest and juice. Fold through the grated carrot, beansprouts and chilli. Season.

4 Serve two crab nests each with the coleslaw on the side.

Stuffed acorn squash

Serves 4

507 calories per serving

Takes 20 minutes to prepare,
50 minutes to cook

4 x 300 g (10½ oz) acorn
squashes

200 g (7 oz) dried mixed wild
and basmati rice

50 g (1¾ oz) flaked almonds

a small bunch of fresh parsley,
chopped finely

1 garlic clove, crushed

4 ripe tomatoes, de-seeded and
chopped finely

25 g (1 oz) ready to eat dried
apricots, chopped

20 stoned black olives in brine,
drained and chopped

grated zest and juice of a lemon

salt and freshly ground black
pepper

*Celebrate autumn with these lovely little individual
stuffed squashes.*

1 Preheat the oven to Gas Mark 5/190°C/fan oven 170°C.
Wash the squashes and pierce in several places with the tip
of a knife. Bake for 30 minutes, until tender. Remove from
the oven and leave until cool enough to handle.

2 Meanwhile, bring a saucepan of water to the boil, add the
rice and cook for 10–15 minutes until tender. Drain. Heat a
small non stick frying pan, add the flaked almonds and toast
until golden. Be careful not to let them burn.

3 Slice a lid off the top of each squash and keep to one side.
Scoop out the seeds and discard. Scoop out some pulp from
the centres but leave a thick shell. If the bottom is not flat,
cut a thin slice off to make a firm base.

4 Roughly chop the pulp and place in a bowl. Add all the
other ingredients, including the cooked rice and toasted
almonds, and stir together. Pile back into the squashes and
replace the lids on top of the filling.

5 Place the squashes in a shallow ovenproof dish and bake
for 20 minutes, until golden.

Tip... When choosing acorn squash, look for one that is
heavy with smooth dull skin and no soft spots. Look for
orange on the skin as this tells you it's mature and ready
to use – but too much orange means it is over ripe.

Salmon, mussel and noodle stew

Serves 4

189 calories per serving

Takes 10 minutes to prepare,
20 minutes to cook

1 large leek, sliced

a bunch of spring onions, sliced finely

1 garlic clove, chopped finely

600 ml (20 fl oz) vegetable stock

50 g (1¾ oz) dried vermicelli or thread egg noodles

175 g (6 oz) salmon fillet

450 g (1 lb) mussels in shells, scrubbed

150 ml (5 fl oz) skimmed milk

salt and freshly ground black pepper

2 tablespoons chopped fresh flat leaf parsley, to garnish

This easy fish dish tastes superb and you can cook it all in one pan.

1 Put the leek, spring onions, garlic and stock into a large lidded saucepan. Bring to the boil, reduce the heat and simmer for 5 minutes.

2 Add the vermicelli or egg noodles and sit the whole salmon fillet on top. Cover and cook gently for 5 minutes. Lift the salmon from the pan and leave to cool for a few minutes.

3 Meanwhile, check the mussels, discarding any that are damaged or remain open when tapped. Add to the saucepan, cover and simmer for 2–3 minutes until the shells open (discard any that remain shut).

4 Flake the salmon, discarding the skin and any bones. Return to the saucepan with the milk and reheat gently. Season to taste and then serve, sprinkled with the parsley.

Beef and mushroom fried rice

Serves 4
308 calories per serving
Takes 30 minutes

150 g (5½ oz) dried brown rice
300 g (10½ oz) lean beef mince
calorie controlled cooking
   spray
250 g (9 oz) mushrooms, sliced
   if large
2 garlic cloves, crushed
110 g (4 oz) beansprouts
60 g (2 oz) dark green cabbage,
   shredded finely
1 egg, beaten
2 tablespoons soy sauce
salt and freshly ground black
   pepper

*The economy packs of mushrooms available in
supermarkets are ideal for this recipe.*

1 Bring a large saucepan of water to the boil, add the rice
and cook according to the packet instructions. Drain.

2 Meanwhile, heat a wok or non stick frying pan until hot,
add the beef and stir fry for 8–10 minutes until crispy – you
will need to do this at a high heat. Remove from the pan,
season and set aside. Keep warm.

3 Lightly spray the same pan with the cooking spray, add the
mushrooms and cook for 5–7 minutes until the juices have
evaporated and the mushrooms are beginning to brown. Add
the garlic, beansprouts and cabbage. Stir fry for 2–3 minutes
until the cabbage is wilted and then add the rice, egg and soy
sauce. Cook, stirring, for 1–2 minutes until hot and the egg
is cooked.

4 Serve the rice on warmed plates topped with the crispy
beef.

Simple sushi

Serves 4
245 calories per serving
Takes 55 minutes

200 g (7 oz) dried sushi rice, rinsed and
  drained
3 tablespoons rice vinegar
1 tablespoon artificial sweetener
½ teaspoon salt
4 sheets seaweed
4 pea sized 'blobs' of wasabi paste, plus
  extra to serve
10 cm (4 inches) cucumber, peeled and cut
  into thin lengths

½ celery stick, cut into long strips
3 crab sticks, each cut in half lengthways
6–8 thin strips of red or yellow pepper
6 asparagus spears, tinned or lightly cooked

To serve
pickled ginger
soy sauce

If you haven't tried sushi before, these simple rolls are a great introduction to Japanese cuisine. They make a great talking point as a starter for a dinner party.

1 Place the rice in a lidded heavy based saucepan with 250 ml (9 fl oz) of water. Bring to the boil and simmer for 10 minutes, stirring occasionally to prevent it sticking together. Remove from the heat, cover and leave to stand for 15 minutes.

2 Meanwhile, make your sushi vinegar by mixing together the rice vinegar, sweetener and salt.

3 Put the cooked rice into a large non metallic bowl and use a plastic spatula to break up any lumps. Gradually pour in the rice vinegar and continue to slice through the rice for 2–3 minutes to cool it a little. The rice should be sticky but not lumpy.

continues overleaf ▶

4 Place a sheet of seaweed, shiny side down, on a clean tea towel. Use damp hands to pick up a quarter of the rice and place it in the middle of the seaweed. Dampening your hands regularly, flatten the rice and spread it towards you so that it is about 2 cm (¾ inch) from the edge of the seaweed closest to you and up the sides. At the end it will be several centimetres from the back of the seaweed and about ½ cm (¼ inch) thick.

5 Put a pea size blob of wasabi paste on your finger and wipe it from right to left along the rice, about 5 cm (2 inches) from the edge nearest you. Lay strips of cucumber along the wasabi. For the crabstick rolls, lay the strips of celery and crab sticks alongside; for the vegetarian rolls, lay the strips of red pepper and asparagus spears alongside. Trim any long ends later.

6 To roll the sushi, start with the edge nearest to you. Lift up the tea towel and ease the seaweed into a roll. You might have to tuck in the fillings and uncovered seaweed. Continue to roll until all the seaweed has been wrapped around the filling.

7 Move the roll to a board and trim the ends with a sharp knife. Cut the roll into six smaller ones and repeat for the rest of the seaweed.

8 Arrange three of each type of roll on a plate and garnish with extra wasabi, pickled ginger and a dipping bowl of soy sauce.

Tip... This recipe makes 24 rolls.

Oriental cod and noodles

Serves 4

556 calories per serving

Takes 5 minutes to prepare
+ 30 minutes marinating,
10 minutes to cook

**4 x 200 g (7 oz) skinless cod
steaks**

For the marinade

4 tablespoons soy sauce

2 tablespoons honey

**4 tablespoons rice wine or
white wine vinegar**

For the stir fry

250 g (9 oz) dried noodles

**calorie controlled cooking
spray**

1 teaspoon sesame oil

**a bunch of spring onions, cut
diagonally into 2.5 cm (1 inch)
lengths**

**a head of broccoli, cut into
florets**

**2 tablespoons toasted sesame
seeds**

*The cod remains moist on the inside while the outside is
crisp. It's richly flavoured with soy and honey and served
on a bed of stir fried noodles with broccoli.*

1 Stir the marinade ingredients together in a shallow dish.
Add the cod steaks and leave to marinate for up to 30 minutes
in the fridge.

2 Meanwhile, bring a saucepan of water to the boil, add the
noodles and cook according to the packet instructions. Drain,
rinse and drain again. Preheat the grill to high.

3 Remove the cod steaks from the marinade, reserving the
marinade, and place under the grill for about 5 minutes on
each side or until cooked through.

4 Meanwhile, spray a wok or large non stick frying pan with
the cooking spray and place over a high heat. Add the sesame
oil, spring onions and broccoli and toss for 3 minutes. Add the
noodles, reserved marinade and sesame seeds and stir fry
for a further 5 minutes.

5 Pile the noodles on to serving plates and top each with a
cod steak.

Prawn red curry

Serves 4

239 calories per serving

Takes 20 minutes

2 tablespoons red Thai curry paste

1 green pepper, de-seeded and sliced

150 g (5½ oz) baby corn

½ x 400 ml can reduced fat coconut milk

300 ml (10 fl oz) vegetable stock

150 g (5½ oz) cooked peeled prawns, defrosted if frozen

110 g (4 oz) beansprouts

2 x 150 g packets straight to wok Udon noodles

a handful of chopped fresh coriander, to garnish

Prawns go well with red curry paste, so give this spicy Thai curry a whirl.

1 Heat a large, lidded, non stick saucepan until hot. Add the curry paste, pepper and baby corn. Cook for 2–3 minutes until beginning to brown.

2 Add the coconut milk and stock. Bring to the boil, cover and simmer for 10 minutes.

3 Add the prawns, beansprouts and noodles. Cook for 2–3 minutes until hot and then serve in warmed bowls garnished with the coriander.

Variation…For a fantastic beef version, see the recipe on page 134.

Tuna and wild rice bake

Serves 4

234 calories per serving

Takes 25 minutes to prepare,
20 minutes to cook

❄

225 g (8 oz) dried mixed long
grain and wild rice

calorie controlled cooking
spray

150 g (5½ oz) button
mushrooms, sliced

225 g (8 oz) leeks, sliced

4 celery sticks, sliced

350 g can low fat condensed
mushroom soup

185 g can tuna in brine, drained
and flaked

300 ml (10 fl oz) skimmed milk

1 teaspoon chopped fresh dill
or ½ teaspoon dried dill

50 g (1¾ oz) half fat Cheddar
cheese, grated

salt and freshly ground black
pepper

*Low fat condensed soup makes an excellent and easy
sauce. It adds a rich flavour to this tasty tuna bake.*

1 Bring a saucepan of water to the boil, add the rice and cook
according to the packet instructions. Drain thoroughly.

2 Meanwhile, heat a large non stick saucepan and spray it
with the cooking spray. Add the mushrooms, leeks and celery
and cook them over a medium-low heat, stirring, until the
vegetables have softened.

3 Mix in the mushroom soup, tuna, milk and dill and season.
Add the cooked rice and stir well. Preheat the oven to Gas
Mark 5/190°C/fan oven 170°C.

4 Spoon the rice mixture into an ovenproof dish and top with
the grated cheese. Bake for 20 minutes until the cheese is
melted and bubbling. Serve hot.

*Tip…You can buy long grain rice and wild rice already
mixed together.*

Duck with hoisin noodles

Serves 4

495 calories per serving

Takes 20 minutes to prepare,
54 minutes to cook

**4 x 175 g (6 oz) skinless duck
legs**

**160 g (5¾ oz) dried medium
egg noodles**

**calorie controlled cooking
spray**

12 baby corn, halved

**a bunch of spring onions,
shredded**

4 tablespoons hoisin sauce

**2 tablespoons fresh coriander,
chopped**

**half a small cucumber, cut into
thin sticks**

*This is a take on crispy duck with pancakes, but using
noodles instead.*

1 Bring a large lidded pan of water to the boil, add the duck
legs, cover and simmer for 50 minutes. Drain well and pat
dry with kitchen towel. Preheat the grill to medium and grill
the legs for 3–4 minutes, turning once. This will give a better
colour to the meat and some lovely crispy bits.

2 Meanwhile, bring a large saucepan of water to the boil, add
the noodles and cook according to the packet instructions.
Drain well and set aside.

3 Spray the same pan with the cooking spray and heat until
hot. Add the baby corn, stir fry for 2 minutes and then add
the spring onions and continue cooking for another minute.
Add the hoisin sauce, 150 ml (5 fl oz) of water and the
noodles and warm through gently. Stir in the coriander.

4 To serve, pull the duck meat from the bone and shred it;
it should come away easily. Divide the noodles and vegetables
between four warmed bowls and top with the duck meat and
cucumber sticks.

Nonya noodle curry

Serves 4

388 calories per serving

Takes 15 minutes + marinating
❄

Nonya cooking combines Chinese and Malaysian influences to produce a spicy aromatic flavour.

3 tablespoons light soy sauce

400 g (14 oz) skinless boneless turkey breast, diced

250 g (9 oz) dried egg noodles

calorie controlled cooking spray

1 large carrot, peeled and cut into matchsticks

100 g (3½ oz) sugar snap peas

2 garlic cloves, chopped

2.5 cm (1 inch) fresh root ginger, chopped finely

1 long red chilli, de-seeded and sliced thinly

4 spring onions, sliced on the diagonal

1 tablespoon medium curry powder or garam masala

½ teaspoon turmeric

freshly ground black pepper

1 Put the soy sauce in a shallow dish, add the turkey, turn to coat it in the sauce and set aside for 30 minutes.

2 Meanwhile, bring a saucepan of water to the boil, add the noodles and cook according to the packet instructions. Drain and refresh under cold running water.

3 Drain the turkey, reserving the marinade. Spray a wok or large non stick frying pan with the cooking spray, add the turkey and stir fry for 5 minutes until lightly golden.

4 Add the carrot and sugar snap peas and cook for a further 2 minutes. Stir in the garlic, ginger, chilli and spring onions, followed by the curry powder and turmeric. Cook for 1 minute before adding the reserved marinade and 6 tablespoons of water.

5 Stir in the drained noodles and cook until heated through. Season with pepper.

Chinese special pork rice

Serves 4

492 calories per serving

Takes 1 hour + 1 hour
  marinating

❄

A great Saturday night supper dish.

350 g (12 oz) pork tenderloin
1 tablespoon Chinese five spice
2 tablespoons soy sauce
2 tablespoons tomato ketchup
250 g (9 oz) dried long grain
  rice
calorie controlled cooking
  spray
150 g (5½ oz) carrots, peeled
  and diced finely
100 g (3½ oz) frozen peas
6 spring onions, sliced
150 g (5½ oz) beansprouts
1 egg, beaten

1 Rinse the pork and pat it dry with kitchen towel. Place it in a dish. Mix together the Chinese five spice, soy sauce and tomato ketchup and spoon it over the pork. Leave the pork to marinate for 1 hour.

2 Preheat the oven to Gas Mark 6/200°C/fan oven 180°C. Place the marinated pork in a roasting tin and roast for 40 minutes.

3 Meanwhile, bring a saucepan of water to the boil, add the rice and cook according to the packet instructions. Drain, rinse in cold water and drain again.

4 Using clean hands, gently separate the cooled rice grains. Heat a large non stick frying pan and spray it with the cooking spray. Add the carrots, peas, spring onions and beansprouts and stir fry for 2–3 minutes. Mix the rice into the pan and cook, stirring frequently, for 5 minutes.

5 Push the rice mixture to one side of the pan and pour the egg into the cleared space. Cook, without stirring, until you see the egg setting and then mix the cooked egg into the rice.

6 Using two forks, shred the cooked pork and mix it into the rice. Serve hot.

Oriental mackerel and rice

Serves 1
388 calories per serving
Takes 15 minutes

50 g (1¾ oz) dried long grain rice
4 baby corn, each cut in half
1 tablespoon frozen peas
25 g (1 oz) cooked smoked mackerel fillets with crushed peppercorns
1 spring onion, sliced
½ teaspoon sesame seeds
soy sauce, to taste

Try this dish as a packed lunch and eat cold.

1 Bring a saucepan of water to the boil, add the rice and cook according to the packet instructions. Drain and place in a bowl.

2 Meanwhile, bring a second small saucepan of water to the boil, add the baby corn and peas and cook until tender, 3–4 minutes. Drain and mix with the rice.

3 Remove the skin from the fish and flake the flesh.

4 Top the rice and vegetables with the fish and spring onion. Sprinkle with the sesame seeds and season to taste with the soy sauce.

Quorn fricassee

Serves 4
345 calories per serving
Takes 30 minutes

125 g (4½ oz) dried brown
  basmati rice
calorie controlled cooking
  spray
2 onions, chopped
2 large garlic cloves, chopped
1 red pepper, de-seeded and
  diced
2 teaspoons dried mixed herbs
200 g can sweetcorn, drained
300 g (10½ oz) Quorn Chicken
  Style Pieces
2 large handfuls of fresh
  spinach, washed
200 ml (7 fl oz) vegetable stock
5 tablespoons half fat crème
  fraîche
juice of ½ a small lemon
salt and freshly ground black
  pepper
3 tablespoons chopped fresh
  parsley, to garnish (optional)

*This version of the French creamy stew features Quorn,
which makes a convenient meat alternative. Serve with
colourful vegetables, such as broccoli or carrots.*

1 Bring a saucepan of water to the boil, add the rice and cook
according to the packet instructions.

2 Meanwhile, heat a wok or large, lidded, non stick frying
pan and spray with the cooking spray. Add the onions and
cook, covered, for 5 minutes. Spray again with the cooking
spray and add the garlic, pepper, herbs, sweetcorn and Quorn
pieces. Cook for a further 3 minutes, stirring continuously.

3 Add the spinach and then the stock, crème fraîche and
lemon juice. Season to taste and heat through for about
2 minutes until the spinach has wilted.

4 Serve with the cooked rice and sprinkled with the parsley,
if using.

Rosemary pork skewers with fresh pepper sauce

Serves 4

419 calories per serving

Takes 35 minutes to prepare,
10–15 minutes to cook

3 red peppers, halved and
de-seeded

175 g (6 oz) dried brown rice

110 g (4 oz) green beans,
trimmed and chopped into
10 cm (4 inch) pieces

8 fresh rosemary sprigs, about
20 cm (8 inches) long

400 g (14 oz) pork loin, cubed

1 courgette, cut into rounds and
then halved

calorie controlled cooking
spray

1 tablespoon olive oil

2 teaspoons white wine vinegar

salt and freshly ground black
pepper

Using rosemary sticks for skewers helps to infuse the meat with the full flavour of the herb.

1 Preheat the grill to medium-high. Place the peppers skin side up under the grill for 3–4 minutes until black. Place in a plastic bag and set aside until step 4.

2 Meanwhile, bring a large saucepan of water to the boil, add the rice and cook according to the packet instructions. Add the green beans for the final 4 minutes of cooking time. Drain and cover to keep warm.

3 Turn down the grill to medium. Remove most of the needles from the rosemary sprigs, reserving a tablespoon. Thread the pork cubes and courgette pieces on to the eight rosemary skewers (it's easier if you pierce a hole in the pork with a metal skewer first). Spray with the cooking spray and grill, turning regularly for 10–15 minutes, until cooked through.

4 Take the peppers from the bag. Remove the skin and discard. Roughly chop the peppers, place in a liquidiser or blender and blend to a paste. Add the oil and vinegar with a little seasoning and the reserved rosemary needles and blend again. Serve two skewers each with the rice and beans and the sauce on the side.

☉ Variation... For a vegetarian option, thread 2 x 150 g packets of marinated tofu pieces on to the rosemary skewers instead of the pork.

Egg fried rice

Serves 2
386 calories per serving
Takes 20 minutes

100 g (3½ oz) dried long grain
rice

calorie controlled cooking
spray

6 spring onions, chopped

1 red pepper, de-seeded and
diced

1 garlic clove, crushed

60 g (2 oz) canned sweetcorn,
drained

75 g (2¾ oz) fresh or frozen
peas

8 crab sticks, cut into chunks

1 egg, beaten

1 tablespoon soy sauce

*This a tasty fast dish that is perfect for lunch or as a light
supper.*

1 Bring a saucepan of water to the boil, add the rice and cook
for 15 minutes or according to the packet instructions. Drain.

2 After about 10 minutes, heat a wok or non stick frying pan
and spray with the cooking spray. Add the spring onions,
red pepper and garlic and stir fry for 2 minutes.

3 Add the sweetcorn, peas, crab sticks and cooked rice.
Stir fry for a further minute.

4 Make a space in the bottom of the wok among the
vegetables and pour in some of the egg. Stir it so that it
sets in little pieces and then repeat this pouring and stirring
with the rest of the egg.

5 Mix everything together and serve immediately with a little
soy sauce to taste.

 Variation... For a great vegetarian version, see the
recipe on page 143

Chinese chillied monkfish

Serves 4
220 calories per serving
Takes 20 minutes

calorie controlled cooking
  spray
**4 x 100 g (3½ oz) monkfish
  fillets**
½ tablespoon cornflour
1 spring onion, chopped finely
1 garlic clove, chopped finely
**1 cm (½ inch) fresh root ginger,
  chopped finely**
**½ red pepper, de-seeded and
  sliced thinly**
125 g (4½ oz) dried egg noodles
200 ml (7 fl oz) chicken stock
1 tablespoon tomato purée
½ tablespoon chilli sauce
½ teaspoon salt
1 teaspoon caster sugar

*Monkfish is a lovely meaty fish that holds its shape well
when cooked. It's perfect for stir frying.*

1 Heat a non stick frying pan and spray with the cooking
spray. Coat the fish lightly with the cornflour and fry for
2–3 minutes on each side. Remove from the pan and
keep warm.

2 Spray the pan again, add the spring onion, garlic, ginger
and red pepper and stir fry for 2–3 minutes.

3 Meanwhile, bring a saucepan of water to the boil, add the
noodles and cook for 5 minutes or according to the packet
instructions.

4 Put all the remaining ingredients into a jug and thoroughly
combine. Add them to the vegetables, bring to a simmer and
continue to cook for 5 minutes.

5 Add the cooked fish, heat through for 3 minutes and then
serve immediately with the noodles.

Index